# A Comprehensive Dictionary of Sociological Terms and Concepts With Examples and Review Questions

## Taron McKenzie

## Introduction

This new dictionary includes additional concepts, terms, and names than in the previous version in my continuing effort to make this dictionary fully comprehensive and useful for sociology students. The use of this dictionary is designed to help students master the vocabulary used in the scientific discipline of sociology. I believe that an enhanced understanding of the vocabulary used by sociologists in their quest to discover social facts leads to a better understanding of the discipline by students.

It is not easy to compile a dictionary of sociological terms, concepts, and processes because the discipline is a living discipline unlike some other scientific areas of study. For instance, geologists might discover more components of a rock than previously thought, but the rock is still a rock and has not changed. Sociology on the other hand, by being a living discipline is always evolving—terms, theories, and processes come and go as the discipline adapts to the changing social world. Because of this, this dictionary is ever-changing.

# Part I: Dictionary

**Absolute Monarchy.** A traditional system of authority, it is a political system in which a monarch, a queen or king, exercises total control over his or her dominion.

**Absolute Poverty.** There are two types of poverty measures: relative and absolute. A relative measure of poverty would examine how much any one person or household had in comparison to the average individuals or households had in that society. However, relative poverty might identify someone as poor with an income of $50,000 per year if the mean income for the community or society is $75,000 per year. But can an individual live on $50,000 a year? Of course, and in relative comfort. So that doesn't seem to be the best measure of poverty. What is needed is something that measures how much individuals and families need to survive and that is what an absolute measure of poverty does—it takes into account the costs of those things necessary for survival like food, shelter, medical costs, transportation costs, clothing, and other items. The condition of having too little income to buy the necessities-- food, shelter, clothing, and/or health care is called absolute poverty.

**Academic Discipline.** Different scientific approaches to studying all things that exist in the world. All use the scientific method to discover that world.

**Access.** Referring to minority and underrepresented groups, it is the creating, measuring and redesigning opportunities to enhance their participation in social, economic and political life.

**Accommodation.** According to Gillin and Gillin (1948), 'accommodation is the term used by sociologists to describe a process by which competing and conflicting individuals and groups adjust their relationships to each other in order to overcome the difficulties which arise in competition, contravention or conflict'.

**Acculturation.** Assimilation into a different culture, typically the dominant one.

**Achieved Status.** The position in society one holds as a result of his/her own efforts. This is in opposition to ascribed status where one's position in society is passed down or given to an individual based on some prescribed criteria. For instance, Bill Gates has achieved status (because he earned his money and position) while Carolyn Kennedy has ascribed status (because her father was a US Senator, another uncle was a US Senator, and still another uncle was a president).

**Acquaintance Rape.** Rape that is perpetrated by someone the victim knows. Acquaintances may include someone the victim is dating, a co-worker, a classmate, a step-father, and virtually anyone who is known to the victim.

**Act.** Referring to George Herbert Mead's theory of the development of the "self," there are four components: (1) the actor "receives" an impulse, (2) perceives the stimuli for that impulse, (3) takes action to fulfil the impulse based on the perceived stimuli, and (4) satisfies the initial impulse.

**Action.** Behaviors that people use to achieve some goal resulting from a deliberate and conscious process.

**Actor-Observer Effect.** Associated with the fundamental attribution error, a tendency to attribute a person's own actions to external forces and situations, while attributing other people's behavior, usually those in an outgroup, to internal causes.

**Actors.** Refers to people engaged in some aspect of human social life.

**Activism.** Action taken to solicit support for a candidate or policy that leads to social or political change.

**Adaptation.** In relation to sociology, the term refers to systems theory. A system exists within an environment. Conditions within that environment change periodically as a result of many factors. The primary goal of any system is survival. Adaptation refers to the ability or desire of a system to adapt to changes in the environment so that it can meet its primary goal of survival. In a broader scientific sense, the term refers to the adaptation of species to their environments.

**Adam Smith.** Adam Smith (1723 – 1790) was a Scottish philosopher, but who is known for his work with the political economy. In fact, he is considered the father of the modern free market economy. Smith (right) published his seminal work the Wealth of Nations in which he laid out his idea that reason would guide self-interest in the marketplace and the resulting competition would lead to overall economic prosperity.
Smith also believed that a broader division of labor (i.e., breaking work down into smaller tasks) would lead to greater productivity. He believed this greater

productivity would result in lower prices for consumers and an overall increase in the standard of living for the society.

**Adhocracy.** An informal non-bureaucratic system that is totally responsive to the environment and any changes that may occur. The system is entirely and singularly dedicated to its goals.

**Adorno's Authoritarian Personality Theory.** Theodore Adorno (1903 – 1969) was a German philosopher and sociologist. Because his father was Jewish, he was forced to flee Germany after the Nazis came to power. Adorno's theory suggests personality needs or deficits that exist within people can precipitate the development of prejudice. Adorno believed that children raised in authoritarian homes where there is an absence of love, harshness of discipline, no discussion and freedom of thought, often develop a  lifelong insecurity. Adorno believed as adults this insecurity would manifest itself in repressed anger and rage, which was then projected onto out-groups. Further, he believed that such people tended to be inflexible and have a rigid way of thinking about life; i.e., they found ambiguity difficult to tolerate—to them, the world was simply black or white with no shades of grey. Though criticized for his generalization, Adorno believed that there was something called the "German national character" and that the German people, because of their authoritarian nature, needed to be ruled by an authoritarian "father" because of their need to see the world in simple terms—hence their acceptance of Hitler has their national leader.

**Affective Action.** An emotional reaction. See also, Weber, Max.

**Affirmative Action.** Organizational policies designed to provide for equal opportunities for the employment of minorities.

**Age Discrimination.** Discrimination based on a person's age. Primarily an issue in the labor force.

**Ageism.** First used by Robert Butler in 1969, ageism is prejudice directed at the elderly as a result of generalized stereotypes. Prejudice toward the elderly may result in discrimination in a number of different arenas (e.g., the workplace).

**Agents.** Actors or institutions which have the ability to affect the social world. For instance, agents of socialization refer to those institutions in which socialization occurs. Examples include the family, friends, and the educational system. Change can result from influence or power.

**Agents of Socialization.** Socialization is the life-long process of learning the normative behaviors and attitudes of the groups to which people belong. Central to the process of socialization are the arenas in which socialization occurs—they are called agents of socialization. Those agents include: the family, the educational system, friends, the mass media, the workplace, religion, and the military. See also anticipatory socialization.

**Aggregate.** A research term designating a collection of people who have no common ties but occupy the same space at a static point in time. For instance, a group of people waiting for a bus would be an aggregate. Another term would be congeries.

**Aggression.** An intentional act of causing harm to another individual.

**Aggressive Script.** Aggressive scripts are stereotypical violent actions usually acquired in early childhood, rehearsed and played out mentally from childhood on, and then carried out when the relevant scenario appears.

**Agnosticism.** A belief that does not deny or affirm the existence of a god.

**Agrarian Societies.** Mankind went from hunting and gathering to pastoral and then agrarian societies. In agrarian societies man stayed in one place, rather than being nomadic to differing degrees in the first two societies, to farm and raise livestock. Marx believed this represented the first instances of stratification.

**Acquired Immune Deficiency Syndrome (AIDS).** A disease that attacks the human immune system and is thought to be passed on by unprotected sexual contact and shared needles used by those injecting themselves with illegal drugs.

**Acute Disease.** Generally, chronic diseases are those that are manageable with appropriate drugs, whereas acute diseases are usually short-term in nature and usually fatal.

**Adaptation.** The idea that according to system's theory that systems must adapt to changes in the environment in order to survive.

**Adult Socialization.** Socialization occurs at all stages of the life-course. Adult socialization pertains specifically to those roles learned in adulthood.

**Affirmative Action.** A government program designed to provide equal opportunity in the workplace for minorities and women. All institutions receiving funds from Federal and State governments must comply to these regulations.

**Age Cohort.** Refers to people born during the same general period of time and often share similar characteristics--for instance the generation of Americans who grew-up during the Great Depression, the "Vietnam Generation," the "Baby Boom Generation," the "X Generation," and the "Y Generation."

**Age Discrimination.** Discrimination directed at people because of their age; usually related to the labor force.

**Ageism.** Prejudice and discrimination directed at people of specific age cohorts. Generally, but not always directed at the young and the old.

**Agrarian Society.** A society in which members settle in a specific area, raise crops, reap the benefits of their own labor, and often amass surplus. Societies in the order of their appearance include hunting and gathering, pastoral, agrarian, industrial, and post-industrial. We currently live in a post-industrial society.

**Alger, Horatio.** Horatio Alger (1832 – 1899) wrote a number of highly successful books for young men. The central theme in his books was how through hard work, courage, and dedication any man, regardless how poor they might have been, could achieve wealth and success. His books were called "rags to riches" stories and have inspired Americans for more than a hundred years. The so-called "American dream" is largely based on his novels.
Sociologists continue to expose the "American dream" as largely a myth in that hard work doesn't pay off the same for all who do so.

**Alienation.** People who feel isolated, estranged, and cut off from others; unclear what is expected of them. Marx believed that the movement from agrarian to industrial societies led to people becoming estranged from their work because they no longer directly received the benefits of that work. See also anomie, Durkheim, and Marx.

**Allport's Theory of Contact.** Gordon Allport (1887 – 1967) was an American psychologist who is considered the father of personality psychology. Among his many prominent students, was Stanley Milgram who went on to conduct studies on obedience to authority. When investigating prejudice, Allport believed that if competing groups could be brought together with equal status as they sought to achieve common goals, prejudice would
be reduced. The government largely used his "contact hypothesis" to reduce prejudice by instituting school-bussing (i.e., bussing students from one school to another so that schools were more diverse), housing projects in which low income residents live side by side with people who have higher incomes, and in

the military. Though prejudice still exists in the military, it has been the most successful at using diversity to reduce levels of prejudice. Allport stated that the two groups must meet in the pursuit of common goals as casual contact will not result in any significant reduction in prejudice.

**Altruism.** Motivation to help another person without expecting to be extrinsically rewarded.

**Altruistic Helping.** Altruism is the act of helping others without an expectation they will be rewarded or the act reciprocated. If it truly exists, it would define selflessness. See, Homans' Social Exchange Theory.

**Altruistic Suicide.** Émile Durkheim believed that while being unsure of group or societal rules, what roles they are expected to perform in that group or society, and generally being isolated or estranged from that group can lead to anomie and anomie can result in suicide (i.e., anomic suicide). On the other hand, altruistic suicide exists when people are completely enmeshed in the group to which they are associated and the group leads them to commit suicide or forces them to do so. See, Jim Jones and the People's Temple.

**Amalgamation.** The assimilation of people into one homogenous group that accepts the dominant group's values and behaviors.

**Ambivalent Sexism.** Researchers Glick and Fisk (2016) suggested there were two types of sexism: that which is overt, known as hostile sexism, and one that is more covert, known as ambivalent sexism. It is important to note that both are acts of sexism. While ambivalent sexism may not be hostile or aggressive in nature, it still represents viewing women in terms of cultural stereotypes.

**Americanization.** The spread of American culture around the world.

**American Dream.** Based on the famous 19th century books written by Horatio Alger, it is the belief that all men, regardless of their social position at birth, is capable of success and wealth through the virtue of hard work and thriftiness.

**Androgyny.** People who possess both masculine and feminine characteristics.

**Annulment.** The legal process for declaring a marriage invalid from its inception. If an annulment is granted, legally the marriage is said to have never occurred. Annulments are also granted by religious bodies—most notably the Catholic Church. Divorce is not recognized by the Catholic Church and therefore adherents often seek an annulment of a failed marriage. Under Canon Law, the Catholic Church can declare a marriage invalid or annulled if all the conditions the church requires for a marriage to be legitimate are not met.

**Anomic Suicide.** Émile Durkheim believed that while being unsure of group or societal rules, what roles they are expected to perform in that group or society, and generally being isolated or estranged from that group can lead to anomie and anomie can result in suicide (i.e., anomic suicide). See, Émile Durkheim.

**Anomie.** Anomie is the state of being unclear of social norms; being alienated from other members of the group. Émile Durkheim was the first to use scientific principles in the relatively new science of sociology. He used those principles to study people and groups. Durkheim was the first to advocate that the social world affected people's behaviors. Having identified a concept he called "anomie" (i.e., social estrangement, isolation, feeling lost, and alienated), he sought to study this phenomenon. In the 1800s, Durkheim studied European religions and believed that Catholics experienced less "anomie" than did Protestants. His reasoning was that Catholicism advocated that they approached God as a community and therefore were accountable to God as a community. Protestantism on the other hand, with the Protestant work ethic widely accepted in the Protestant community, believed that they approached God as individuals and were therefore individually accountable to God. Therefore, Durkheim believed that the bonds between Protestants were weaker than they were for Catholics. Based on this premise, Durkheim believed that Protestants would have higher rates of anomie than Catholics. Using scientific principles, he wanted to employ within sociology, he proposed that Protestant countries would have higher rates of anomie than would Catholic countries. To test this, Durkheim reasoned that people who suffered from the effects of anomie would be more likely to commit suicide than others. After finding that Catholic (European) countries reported almost non-existent suicide rates and Protestant (European) countries reporting significantly higher rates, he concluded that his hypothesis had been proven correct: Protestants were more likely to suffer from the effects of anomie. While there were methodological problems with Durkheim's study, he is still credited for being the first to make sociology a science.

**Anomie Theory** (crime). Durkheim's theory that crime occurs when people are unable to achieve norms and goals legitimately by using socially approved means to do so. For instance, college students use approved cultural means (i.e., getting a degree) to obtain socially valued goals (e.g., money, a nice house, a car, nice vacations), but criminals use illegitimate means (i.e., crime) to obtain those socially valued goals. See also, structural strain theory.

**Anticipatory Socialization.** The process of preparing newcomers to become members of an existing social group by helping them to learn the attitudes and behaviors that are considered appropriate before they occupy a particular role. Sometimes we occupy new roles without any preparation for that role (e.g., unemployment), but most of the time we learn and experience some of the norms and behaviors of a role before we occupy that role. For instance, babysitting is a way some young women prepare for the role of mother; dating can serve as anticipatory socialization for marriage.

**Anti-Conformity.** More than just the absence of conformity, it is the conscious and deliberate actions of an individual to oppose conformist attitudes and behaviors.

**Anti-Miscegenation Laws.** Laws that make it a crime to marry or have sex with someone of a different race.

**Anti-Semitism.** Prejudice and discrimination directed at Jews.

**Anxious-Ambivalent Attachment Style.** An attachment style associated with children who separated from a parent for some small period of time, but the stress associated with the parent having left leaves them insecure and sometimes ambivalent when the parent returns. Any attachment style can be carried into adulthood as an emotional issue.

**Apartheid.** A system of segregation formerly in place in the Country of South Africa. Apartheid literally means "to separate." Apartheid ended in 1994.

**Appearance.** The way we appear physically to others. See also, interpersonal attraction.

**Applied Sociology.** The use of sociology for problem solving and that results in practical applications for organizations and governments.

**Applied Research.** Research carried out with the intent of investigating and then offering solutions to institutional or social problems.

**Apprenticeship.** In a guild system, the apprenticeship is the first stage. The apprenticeship is that period when the new member begins to develop the skills they will need to practice their craft and as the same time they learn the norms and values of the guild's culture.

**Archival Research.** Using existing data sources to conduct research. Archival sources can be documents, legal records, and even existing data bases. See, the National Survey of Families and Households conducted by the University of Wisconsin at Madison.

**Arousal--Cost/Reward Model.** Piliavin et al. (1981) proposed that when a person becomes aroused it is often caused by understanding of another person's personal distress, which then leads the aroused person to work to reduce the distress of the other.

**Arranged Marriage.** Marriage which is arranged by parents for purposes of tradition, political ties, or economic considerations.

**Artisan.** A skilled laborer.

**Ascribed Status.** A social position assigned by society and beyond the control of the individual (such as in the case of achieved status). Examples of ascribed statuses would include people who hold a title such as Lord or Queen in monarchical societies. Others are based on race, ethnicity, sex, and age. Queen Elizabeth II of the United Kingdom.

**Assimilation.** Assimilation is the absorption of a minority into the dominant group; acceptance of the norms and values of the majority group by the minority group. Often the following formula is used to illustrate the meaning behind assimilation: $A + B + C = A$ (where A is the dominant group and B and C are minority groups).

**Associations.** The social interactions between people.

**Atheism.** The belief that God does not exist.

**Attachment.** The degree that significant bonds are created between two people--usually between a parent and child.

**Attitude.** A mental orientation resulting from some degree of evaluation and that is held toward some person, object, or experience. Attitudes therefore can be either positive or negative. Explicit attitudes are those that we are conscious of and therefore effect our behavior towards those attitudes, whereas implicit attitudes are unconscious yet still influence our perceptions of others, people's behavior, and our actions. Attitudes are thought to have three components: (1) a cognitive component, or a set of beliefs about the person, object, or experience, (2) an affective component, or how a person feels about the person, object, or experience, and (3) a behavioral component, or a person's tendencies to act in certain ways to the person, object, or experience.

**Attitude-Behavior Link.** Research has consistently found a poor link between expressed attitudes towards an action and the performance of that action. See, Behavioral Intention.

**Attribution.** The process by which people attempt to explain their successes and failures; in other words, the causes of things that affect them. There are two types of attributions: external attribution, where the cause of the behavior or event is perceived to be situational or environmental, and internal, where someone perceives the cause to be internal characteristics--something within or about the person that is beyond their control.

**Audience Inhibition Effect.** Similar to the bystander effect, this theory suggests that people might be reluctant to intervene in an emergency situation.

**Authoritarianism.** A political system where a monarch or dictator rules the country and citizens are not allowed to participate in government. Infamous examples include Henry VIII, Adolf Hitler, Joseph Stalin, Kim Jong Un of North Korea, and Saddam Hussein of Iraq (right).

**Authoritarian Personality.** Associated with Theodore Adorno (1903 - 1969), the authoritarian personality suggests that character flaws are created within people who grow up in strict households, little in the way of love and affection, and harsh discipline. As adults, people who have an authoritarian personality tend to see the world in black and white terms—in other words, they need to see the world simplistically when in fact it is immensely complex and ambiguous. Further, people who have an authoritarian personality are conformists and do not tolerate deviance. The authoritarian personality is highly associated with prejudice.

**Authoritarian State.** There are three accepted components of the authoritarian state: (1) People are excluded from the processes of government, (2) little or no opposition to the government is permitted, and (3) the government has little interest in the lives of its people. Saddam Hussein (right), former dictator of Iraq, headed an authoritarian state while in power.

**Authoritative leadership.** A type of leadership characterized by a strong leader who exhibits total control with little regard for input from others.

**Authority.** Authority is perceived, given, and legitimate. The government has power because it is a legitimate source of authority. There are three types of authority: traditional, legal-rational, and charismatic.

**Autocracy.** Rule by one leader and all power rests in the hands of that leader. An example would be the North Korean (i.e., Democratic People's Republic) ruler Kim Jong-un. Autocratic rule is typified by dictatorships who rule with an iron hand, quash dissention, practice extreme brutality, and intimidate its citizens. Because all power is in the hands of autocrats, they are the state.

**Automation.** Refers to the tendency to replace humans as workers with technology.

**Availability Heuristic.** Immediate thoughts or examples that come to mind when evaluating a novel situation, concept, or decision.

**Aversive Racism.** The theory that when people actively work not to associate with a specific racial or ethnic group they are more likely to develop negative evaluations of that group.

**Avoidant Attachment Style.** One of the four styles of attachment, avoidant attachment style is characterized by fear of emotional closeness in adult relationships.

**Axioms of Science.** All sciences accept that there are axioms that precede the steps of science (the scientific method). Axioms are the "truths" or unquestioned assumptions that pre-exist the steps of science. The following would be regarded as axioms for all sciences:
- Axiom 1: This is a real(ist's) world. A world of "things in themselves" objectively out there whether we can perceive them or not).
- Axiom 2: We can perceive this world. Our five senses allow us to come into contact with "things in themselves").
- Axiom 3: The world is ordered. We can discover order, logic, meaning, explanations, understanding and reason.

**Baby Boom.** America went to war on December 8, 1941 after the Japanese attacked our naval base in Hawaii. Three days later, Adolph Hitler declared war on the US. The war ended in 1945. As American troops came home, coupled with unprecedented economic growth, there occurred what is referred to as the "baby boom," which was a sharp increase in births between 1946 and 1965. This generation is called the "baby boomers."

**Backstage (off-stage).** In Erving Goffman's Dramaturgical Perspective, he believed that people worked to manage the impression others have of them using something called "facework." He believed that like actors, sometimes we are on-stage (also known as front-stage) and sometimes we are off-stage (also known as backstage). When people are on-stage, they work to manage their impression—an activity that constrains them like an actor on stage playing a part. And like an actor, we manage our on-stage impression differently as the people we are around varies. Goffman believed that because on-stage activities were exhausting, people need time in which they can come off-stage where they can relax and recoup. It is while off-stage people can be at ease and think about their performance while on-stage and decide if there is improvement their on-stage self needs to make. See also, off-stage.

**Balance Theory.** See, Heider's balance theory.

**Barter.** A type of economic exchange where people negotiate the exchange of goods. These exchanges are non-monetary.

**Basic Research.** Research conducted to broaden the understanding and knowledge about some phenomena. The goal of pure or basic research is simply to add to the body of knowledge already known about something, whereas applied research attempts to use the knowledge provided by that research to solve some social or organizational problem.

**Battered Women.** Term that refers to women who are physically abused by their partner. See also, domestic abuse.

**Battered Women's Syndrome.** Psychological and physical harm in women who have been victims of emotional, psychological, and physical abuse for an extended period of time. Research has found a clear pattern in the abuse of women by their partners and over time the abuse escalates and the severity increases. In the beginning, the abuse tends to be more verbal, but in time the abuse becomes physical. In the early stages of physical abuse, the male partner often apologizes for the abuse, but as time goes by and the violence gets worse, the apologies stop. Research shows that the longer an abuse victim stays in the relationship, the more likely she will suffer serious injuries. It is typical for a male abuser to blame his victim for the abuse—e.g., "I told her I wanted dinner on the table at 5:30 p.m. when I walked in the door, but she just wouldn't listen so I had to punish her." On average, it takes six attempts for a woman to leave her abusive spouse before she is successful on the seventh, but until she leaves, she inadvertently reinforces the abuse because the abuser sees the abuse as effective and it steadily gets worse. Generally, the trigger that starts abused woman thinking about leaving is when they begin to feel that their life is in danger. While there are a number of reasons given as to why abused women stay in these abusive relationships, the two most often stated are "I still loved him" and "I just wanted him to stop... and really thought things would get better." Estimates suggest that as many as two million women may be physically abused each year by their partners. Psychological harm to battered women includes low self-esteem (often directly resulting from her partner telling her she is unattractive, can't do anything right, and no one else would want her), depressed, anxious, withdrawn (made worse by abusers who often limit their partner's activities outside the home to limit those who might see evidence of the abuse and additionally encourage the battered woman to leave). Because they are hidden away, and because the abuser controls virtually everything including finances, battered women often don't know how to live on their own—they find it difficult to cope with situations that most people find a routine of daily life. Sadly, the research also suggests that the parents of the battered woman encouraged her to be compliant and dependent as a child.

**Baudrillard, Jean.** Jean Baudrillard (1929 – 2007) was a French sociologist who investigated the role of consumerism in post-modern life. Unlike Marx, Baudrillard believed that consumer was much more important when examining the social world than was production as Marx had proposed. Baudrillard advocated that need or perceived need preceded production. He identified four components necessary for the formation of needs: (1) the  functional or utilitarian value of an object, (2) the economic value of the object, (3) the symbolic value of the object, and (4) the relative value of the object to other socially desirable objects.

**Beck, Ulrich.** Ulrich Beck (1944 – 2015) was a German sociologist known for his work on modernization and globalization. He and Anthony Giddens coined the term "risk society" to refer to the postmodern tendency to create risks that people are forced to face and fear. See also, Giddens, Anthony.

**Behavioral Intention.** There is a poor link between an attitude towards some action and the performance of that action; just because some says they like a particular political candidate doesn't mean they will go to the polls on election day and vote for him or her. Fishbein (top right) and Ajzen (below right) developed a model to better predict the link between an attitude and behavior. They believed that behavioral intentions are made up of (1) positive and negative feelings about performing the behavior, and (2) the perceptions a person has about what others will think of the behavior--in other words, is the behavior appropriate or not. Fishbein and Ajzen's theory yields a significantly better ability to predict behavior based on an expressed attitude.

**Behaviorism.** The study of behavior. Behaviorism asks the question: why do people do what they do? A theoretical orientation that draws attention to observed behaviors free of thoughts or feelings and recognizes the influence of environmental factors.

**Beliefs.** The shared ideas and ideals of a cultural group. Usually believed be true.

**Bell, Daniel.** Daniel Bell (1919 – 2011) was an American sociologist known for his studies on post-industrialism. His most influential books are The End of Ideology (1960), The Cultural Contradictions of Capitalism (1976) and the Coming of Post-Industrial Society (1973).

**Bernard, Jessie.** Jessie Bernard (1903 – 1996) (right) was an American sociologist known for her work on the effects of sexism on women's experience of marriage, parenting, education and economic life. She advocated that marriage, while something that benefitted men, was harmful to women.

**Bias.** Bias is a research term indicating scientific error; the inappropriate influence of a researcher's personal interests and beliefs on scientific research.

- For example, pharmaceutical researchers are working on the development of a new drug to combat cancer. They have been promised a huge cash bonus if the drug trials support that the drug will indeed combat cancer. In research, it implies that researchers are more likely to see what they want to see and not necessarily what the research tells them. Another criticism suggests that because researchers are human, it is impossible to eliminate bias when researchers are doing research on other humans.

**Bicultural.** Someone who understands and is able to practice the norms and behaviors of more than one culture is considered to be bicultural.

**Bilateral Kinship.** Where kinship of both parents is considered important in understanding the heritage of a person.

**Binuclear (family).** Children who, because of divorce, are members of two nuclear families—that of their remarried mother and remarried father. Right, picture of binuclear family.

**Biological Determinism.** The belief that biology is responsible for social behavior.

**Biological Drives.** The belief that all human physiological needs reduce to needs for (a) food, (b) water, (c) sex, and (d) love and affection.

**Bioterrorism.** The threat of chemical or biological attack by radical groups to kill and upend a social system.

**Birth Rate.** The birth rate is the number of live births per 1000 per year.

**Birth cohort.** The number of people born in a specific year.

**Birthrates.** The average number of children born to women in a given year.

**Blackface.** Stage makeup used that exaggerates racial stereotypes used to ridicule African people and their descendants in stage presentations.

**Black Feminist Theory.** Theoretical framework which asserts that there are cultural differences that women across the globe experience and the effect is to keep women in their second class positions.

**Blended Family.** A family consisting of two parents and children that resulted from previous marriages (i.e., a step-family).

**Blue-Collar.** Generally, referred to as the working class.

**Blumer, H.** Harold Blumer (1900 – 1987) is credited for providing the name symbolic interaction to the theory devised by George Herbert Mead. Blumer (right) believed that humans create their own social reality by shared interactions and these shared interactions are continuous and ongoing.

**Body Esteem.** One's self-evaluation of their appearance.

**Body Language.** Body movement is often interpreted in our society. The way someone stands, folds their arms, crosses their legs, or even slouches-all our actions that are interpreted. An example, in our culture, would be the interpretation of someone as being closed off or defensive if they were to sit or stand with their arms crossed.

**Bogardus Social Distance Scale.** There are a number of ways researchers can attempt to measure prejudice toward an outgroup, but none are accepted as conclusive evidence—largely because people tend not to consider their own biases toward people unlike them as "prejudice" and therefore provide data that is questionable or outright biased.

**Emory Bogardus** (1882 – 1973) created what is called the Bogardus social distance scale. The scale is designed to measure how close people are willing to accept social contact with members of an outgroup (i.e., members of a racial or ethnic group different from themselves). The scale asks people how comfortable they would feel with a member of an outgroup within a measured proximity to them. It is a cumulative scale, so agreement with one item implies agreement with all preceding statements.

- They should be denied entry into my country
- As non-citizens of my country
- As citizens of my country
- As co-workers at my place of employment
- As neighbors on the same street
- As my close personal friends
- As close relatives by marriage

**Born again.** A Christian concept held by some religions that one must vocally accept Jesus Christ as savior in order to enter heaven. Generally associated with fundamentalist Christian religions.

**Bourgeoisie.** Refers to Marx's conflict perspective. The more widely used term for bourgeoisie is the "haves" or the "owners." See, the conflict perspective.

**Branch Davidians.** A religious group resulting from a schism in the Seventh Day Adventist Church. Branch Davidians believed that the second-coming of Jesus Christ would be within their lifetime. In recent times, the Branch Davidians were led by a man named David Koresh (right) who believed he was Jesus Christ who had come to earth for the day of judgement. The Branch Davidians felt  threatened by their surroundings and in particular the government, so they began to amass stockpiles of weapons—some of which were illegal to possess without proper licensing. In 1993, Koresh received word that he was about to be raided by the A.T.F. (i.e., Alcohol, Tobacco, and Firearms) division of the government and prepared to resist the raid. Escalating rapidly, the event led to a 51-day siege of the Branch Davidian compound by the A.T.F., the F.B.I., the National Guard, and local law enforcement. The siege ended with the deaths of 82 Branch Davidians and four A.T.F. agents. A thorough investigation revealed that the Branch Davidians had set fires in four locations throughout the compound and therefore they were responsible for the vast majority of deaths. See also, McVeigh, Timothy.

**Bridewealth.** Goods and services provided by men to a new bride in exchange for the sole right to her sexual services and offspring.

**Buddhism.** A religion having evolved from Hinduism. Buddhism adheres to the teachings of Siddhartha Gautama, or Buddha (563/480 CE to 483/400 BCE), who believed that the source of human suffering was craving. Buddhism follows the Four Noble Truths and the Eightfold Path.

**Bullying.** Bullying is intentional, aggressive and intimidating behavior directed at school children usually by other children. Many actions constitute bullying, such as spreading rumors, making threats, physical intimidation, physical attacks, and stealing. Sometimes bullying occurs on social media sites. Research reports that approximately three million children stay home from school each month because of bullying. Further, 20% of children who are victims of cyberbullying think about suicide and 10% actually attempt suicide due to bullying.

**Bureaucracy.** Large organizations that often appear as rigid and inefficient, though while often rigid, bureaucratic processes that are adhered to make bureaucracies highly efficient at routine tasks. Characteristics of bureaucracies include: impersonality, promotions based on performance, a clear division of labor, a formal and top-down chain of command, specialization of work tasks, centralized authority, and written rules and procedures.

**Bureaucratization.** Based on Weber's idea of rationalization and bureaucracies, the tendency of modern bureaucracies to increasingly become more and more efficient as they attempt to reach their goals.

**Bystander Effect.** A social psychological behavior in which people are less likely to come to the aid of someone in distress when other people are present.

**Bystander Intervention Model.** A theory proposed by Darley and Latane (1968) that offers an explanatory model of how people can respond positively to situations when people are in distress or in need of help. The theory is proposed as an alternative to the tendency for people to experience the bystander effect. Stage one, notice potentially problematic situations. Stage two, identify when it's appropriate to intervene. Stage three, recognize personal responsibility for intervention. Stage four, know how to intervene. Stage five, take action to intervene.

## The Bystander Intervention Model

1. Notice that something is happening
2. Interpret the event as an emergency
3. Take responsibility for providing help
4. Decide how to provide help
5. Take Action to provide help

**Capitalism.** An economic system where the means of production is owned by private individuals who reap profits from the labor of their workers. This is in opposition to socialism where the means of production is owned by the state (i.e., the people) and prices and profits are tightly regulated.

**Capitalist Class.** The elite of a given society. Using Marx's analogy, those who own the means of production; the rich and powerful who control society through laws resulting from the use of their power that is derived from their wealth.

**Cash-Crop Production.** The production of crops to be sold or traded on the world market rather than for the survival needs of the population that is responsible for growing the crops. During the 1930s, Joseph Stalin, dictator of the Soviet Union, was responsible for the deaths of millions of Ukrainians when he confiscated their crops and sold them on the world market to raise money for his industrialization of the cities.

**Caste System.** In a caste system, there is virtually no possibility for people to move upwards to a higher-ranking caste. While the caste system is officially

'illegal' in India, like everything else, systems in which people were raised are often difficult to change and therefore the caste system is essentially still in existence. There are seven castes with the "untouchables" at the bottom and the "Brahmin" or priestly caste at the top. The caste system is largely tied to Hinduism which advocates that you can be reincarnated to a higher caste if you do good and earn karma in your former life.

**Category.** Common characteristics shared by a group of people but who have nothing else in common.

**Categorization.** The cognitive process by which humans tend to think of people in terms of categories. Categorization is associated with stereotyping and both are associated with prejudice.

**Catharsis.** The purging of negative emotions. For instance, helping others in some way after the death of a loved one might be cathartic.

**Cathedrals of Consumption.** A term coined by American sociologist George Ritzer (right) to describe the process of enticing and enchanting the consumer through "awe and wonder." Examples include massive shopping centers, sports stadiums, amusement parks, and casinos.

**Causality.** Causality is the relationship of cause and effect. If two variables are correlated with another, the question of causality needs to be addressed. Correlations by themselves cannot establish causality. To establish causality the independent variable must precede the dependent variable and be a necessary or sufficient cause of the dependent variable. For instance, in biology it has been proven that smoking causes cancer. When smokers and non-smokers are compared on rates of cancer, it is obvious that smokers are at significantly higher risk of developing cancer; that is enough to allow us to say smoking is a sufficient cause of cancer. And among our sample of smokers, they started smoking before they developed cancer. Consequently, doctors today would agree with the statement that smoking causes cancer.

**Centralization.** Often associated with Communism, a system where power and authority is concentrated into a limited number of offices or agencies.

**Census.** A census is a count of a population and additionally designed to collect demographic data about the population.

**Central Route to Persuasion.** There are two routes to persuasion: the central route, which uses information and reason, and peripheral, which is usually an appeal to emotions.

**Channels of Communication.** Symbolic ways of interpreting meaning within a specific context. They are made up of:

- Verbal symbols:
  - Language: The words we speak.
  - Paralanguage: The way the words are spoken. Accent: People using a New York accent are often thought to be rude and distant, while people using a Southern accent are often thought to be stupid or a redneck. Shaking or quivering voice: Generally, a shaky voice is interpreted as nervousness or fear.

**Charisma.** Personal charm that is used by someone to influence others.

**Charismatic Authority.** Authority that is based on an individual's personal charm and ability to persuade others to his or her beliefs.

**Charismatic Leader.** Someone who has a highly gregarious personality and is able to use that exceptional personality to affect change in others is considered charismatic. Successful politicians, well-known religious leaders, and cult leaders, such as Jim Jones (right) usually have a high degree of charisma that they use to their advantage. Cult leaders often exhibit high levels of charismatic appeal to their followers such as Jim Jones, who as the leader of a cult, was responsible for the deaths of over 900 of his followers.

**Charter Schools.** A charter is a document outlining the rights, privileges, and boundaries of a school. Charters often exist between school administrators, including a school board, those who work in the system (e.g., teachers), and the parents of children attending the school. Though charter schools receive tax revenue, they are not bound to local and state regulations.

**Checks and balances.** A structural feature of government in the United States where all three branches of government--legislative, executive, and judicial are dependent upon one another to carry out their assigned duties.

**Chronic Disease.** Generally, chronic diseases are those that are manageable with appropriate drugs, whereas acute diseases are usually short-term in nature and usually fatal.

**Church.** A large formal organization, it is universal in that all members of society are expected to belong to that church, it is formally allied with the state, eliminates religious competition (see, heresy). In the past, the Catholic

Church would have been regarded as a church in some countries, but where today there is religious pluralism, it now a denomination. In countries where the Catholic Church is still allied with the state, it is a church, e.g., Republic of Ireland, because there is little pluralism.

**Citizen.** A member of a political system, who because of that membership, has both rights and responsibilities.

Citizens United. In a 2010 Supreme Court decision, corporations were judged to have the same rights to free speech as private individuals. The result is the ability for large corporations to contribute unlimited amounts of money to the political campaigns of the candidates whom they support.

**Civil Disobedience.** The active refusal of a people to obey specific laws or policies that are contrary to their best interest. Civil disobedience implies non-violence. While many think that the act was created by Mahatma Gandhi, when he resisted British colonialism of India, historical records indicate that its earliest use was in ancient Greece. Dr. Martin Luther King, Jr. used civil disobedience as a way to protest segregation in the South.

**Civil Disorder.** When a government must intervene to restore order during periods of social unrest.

**Civil Inattention.** Erving Goffman (1922 – 1982) identified something he called civil inattention that we use in our daily lives. As we enter into each other's interpersonal space, we acknowledge the other person briefly with eye contact. So, imagine walking in one direction on a sidewalk and someone is walking towards you in the other direction. Goffman suggests that for one brief part of a second both parties will acknowledge each other by making eye contact. Why does  Goffman (above, right) think this is symbolic? Imagine the same situation where you're walking on the sidewalk in one direction and someone is walking towards you in the other direction and as you lift your eyes to make eye contact with them you notice that their eyes are glued to the sidewalk. As you get closer and closer to each other you notice through your peripheral vision with the other party never looks up from the sidewalk. If eye contact is symbolic in this situation how might you interpret the fact that they never make eye contact with you even though you are entering their space? Might you think that they are distracted? Or maybe they have low self-esteem? What if as they walked toward you on the sidewalk you noticed that not only did they make eye contact with you briefly, but they held it-they stared at you the whole time they passed you. How would you interpret that? Is that aggressive? Is that sexual interest? One way or another you will interpret the meaning of that eye contact.

**Civil Rights.** Legal rights that are guaranteed under law to all citizens of a given society.

**Civil Rights Movement.** Though slavery had officially been abolished in January of 1863, and made policy when the defeated Southern states re-entered the Union in 1865, the 100-year period between 1865 and 1964 saw Southern states adhering to an official policy of segregation. The Civil Rights Movement was a widespread national movement to eliminate segregation and raise African-Americans to the status, rights, and privileges held by white Americans. See also, King, Rev. Dr. Martin Luther, Jr.

**Christianity.** World's largest religion, but began as a cult around Jesus Christ who is the central figure. Today there are hundreds of Christian denominations.

**Clan.** An extended group of kin.

**Class.** The social position one holds in a society that uses a class system (e.g., capitalism). In a class system, people may improve their class position through education, experience, income, occupational prestige, and the accumulation of wealth. The number of classes in the U.S. is largely arbitrary.

**Class conflict.** Associated with Karl Marx. Marx believed that capitalist society would reduce to two classes: those that owned the means of production and those that worked for those who owned the means of production—i.e., the haves versus the have-nots. Marx believed that a two-class system would lead to class conflict as they competed for resources.

**Class Consciousness.** In a class system, the awareness of being in the same mistreated group (i.e., the have-nots) with others can lead to what Marx referred to as class consciousness. Marx believed that class consciousness was necessary to unite the have-nots so that they rebelled against the haves and brought about social change or revolution. See, class conflict.

**Classical Conditioning.** A theory proposed by John Watson (1924) that human actions were simply the result of stimulus provoking a response much in the same way Pavlov's ringing a bell resulted in a dog salivating at the thought of food, which was the result of the bell serving as the stimulus that evoked the response of the dog salivating. Watson believed that the wide variation in human responses to specific stimuli were the result of differences in life-long experiences.

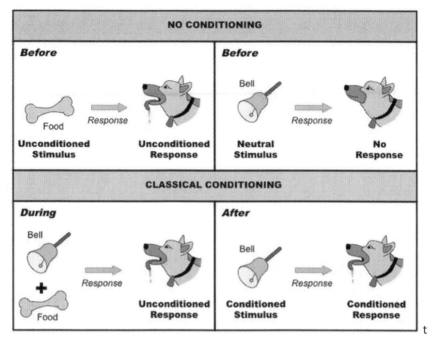

**Classism.** Prejudice and discrimination based on social class; the idea that certain classes of people are superior.

**Class System.** A class system is built on the notion of stratification. A highly stratified system would have only two classes according to Karl Marx: the haves and the have-nots. A class system is characterized the unequal distribution of wealth and property. Though a stratified system like the caste system, in a class system people have the ability to change their class position to varying degrees.

**Clergy.** In an estate system of stratification, those that held the middle position were church officials--Roman Catholic priests and bishops.

**Clerical Worker.** Low-wage workers primarily female performing office tasks.

**Climate Change.** Theory that the earth's temperature is rising due to greenhouse gases (i.e., carbon dioxide and methane), which reflect the sun's rays back to earth and its atmosphere.

**Clinical Sociology.** Clinical sociology involves using sociology to investigate social relationships within an organization or social structure and then developing a plan to alter those relationships so that the system functions with greater cohesion and efficiency.

**Clique.** A small group of people within a larger group of people who share something in common that sets them apart from the others and is usually associated with a feeling of elitism.

**Closed system.** In organizational theory and systems theory, a system is either open to its environment or closed.

**Coalition.** A government where the major political parties unite to form a majority for voting purposes.

**Coercion.** There are four types of social interaction: exchange, collaboration, competition, and coercion. Coercion involves using force or intimidation to get someone to do what you want.

**Coercive Organization.** A formal organization that uses force to create a strict environment of rules and regulations.

**Cognition.** Human thought processes, including perceiving, reasoning, and remembering.

**Cognitive Ability.** In order to solve problems, humans need abstract thinking skills or also known as cognitive abilities.

**Cognitive Development.** Primarily a psychological term, it is the development of the ability of children to think, learn, and understand.

**Cognitive Development Theory.** Jean Piaget (right) proposed that childhood is a time when children begin to acquire knowledge, develop intelligence, and construct their understanding of reality. Piaget believed that children's understanding of reality changed over time as they experienced situations that contradicted their previous understanding.

**Cognitive Dissonance.** An inconsistency between cognitive elements the result of which produces a state of discomfort. The discomfort in turn may lead to attitudinal or behavioral change. For instance, an environmental activist wants a big SUV because of his family, but his values towards environmentalism are incongruent with buying a big gas-guzzling vehicle so he ends up experiencing cognitive dissonance. The dissonance might lead him to buy a smaller SUV or to justify the larger SUV in some way, but the end result is that he has a need to reduce his level of discomfort or cognitive dissonance.

**Cognitive Sociology.** The study of the effects of society on the thought process of individuals.

**Cohabitation.** Couples who live together without marrying but love each other and have some degree of commitment to the relationship. Many couples who cohabitate in the US do so as a trial marriage. However, research shows that couples who cohabitated prior to marrying were more likely to divorce.

**Cohort.** Cohort is a research term that refers to people who are in the same age group or period. For instance, we could talk about the baby-boomers as a cohort, or people in their 20s, or people who grew-up during the Great Depression.

**Colonialism.** The invasion and dominance by one country of a lesser developed country in order to exploit the latter country's resources.

**Collective Action.** Generally, spontaneous social action by people of a society as a result of social or political events.

**Collective Behavior.** Behaviors that are often displayed in crowds, mobs, and riots and involves a perception of self-anonymity and the suspension of norms.

**Collective Conscience.** The shared ideas by the members of a group that guide social behavior.

**Collective Consciousness.** The language, feeling rules, morals, values, beliefs, and scripts of a group or society.

**Collective Identity.** A person's sense of connection with a larger community or group.

**Collective Violence.** Mass violent group behavior resulting from some social, environmental, or political event.

**Collectivism.** Western cultures tend to value human individualism--the individual competing with others or the environment. Collectivism is the opposite of individualism. Collectivism is the ideology that the good of the many outweigh the good of the few. Collectivism values strong bonds between people who help each other because of the communal nature of their relationship to each other.

**Colonialism.** The process of a large industrialized country invading and then occupying a smaller country in order to use their resources for the larger country's economic gain.

**Coming Out.** The formal declaration to others of a person's gay sexuality.

**Commercialism.** Organizational systems that work to ingrain their products into a culture with the organizations ultimate goal of making a profit of those products.

**Commodification.** In a free-market economy goods and services are exchanged en masse where in earlier societies goods and services were exchanged within primary groups.

**Commodity Fetishism.** Marxist concept referring to social relations in complex capitalist societies. Refers to material objects being treated with the same devotion and reverence as if it were sacred.

**Commoners.** In an estate system of stratification commoners were in the lowest strata and who worked for the upper strata.

**Communication.** Information that is transmitted between people.

**Communism.** The politicization of Marx's ideas of socialism in which the means of production was owned by the people, which really mean the state, and supposedly all profits were shared equally among the masses. As a political system, associated with the most brutal dictators in modern history--Vladimir Ilyich Lenin (right) and Joseph Stalin. With the fall of the Soviet Union in 1991, there are only three Communist states remaining in the world--the  People's Republic of China, the People's Republic of North Korea, and the Republic of Cuba. Though the People's Republic of China is still technically a Communist state, it is regarded more as a hybrid due to extensive economic and political reform in the last several decades.

**Community.** Implies a group of people living together, or whose ideals are shared with others, and therefore share bonds and are cohesive.

**Commuter Marriage.** Sometimes marital partners are forced by their jobs or careers to maintain two households. These marital partners live apart during the week but will commute to one or the other's residence on weekends. Generally, commuter marriages are associated with marital partners who are more highly educated and have higher income careers.

**Companionate Love.** A type of love characterized by deep affection, caring, understanding, and selflessness.

**Comparable worth.** Relates to gender inequality. Generally, women are paid less in wages than are men performing the same duties. Comparable worth suggests that men and women should be paid equally when performing the same duties and tasks.

**Competition.** There are four types of social interaction: exchange, collaboration, competition, and coercion. Competition is a form of interaction where people compete for resources.

**Compliance.** Obedience to others who either force their authority on others (i.e., illegitimate authority) or who have legitimate authority over others.

**Comte, Auguste.** Auguste Comte (1798 – 1857) is considered to be the father of sociology because he coined the term sociology. Comte believed that his new science could serve humanity by using scientific principles to study mankind, from that study the ability to predict human behavior would emerge, and this information used to improve humanity. The development of positivism, a view that science could discover social facts, is credited to Comte.

**Concept.** Concepts are research terms that refer to and define what is being studied. Many things can be concepts. For instance, education, income, wealth, poverty, prejudice. Concepts are often variables.

**Conditioning.** Changes in behaviors that follow the presentation of new stimuli. Classical conditioning is when new stimuli becomes linked to a previous stimulus. For instance, a dog knows it's about to be fed when it hears a can opener, but can learn it's about to be fed when another stimulus replaces the former--say hearing or seeing its owner pick up the dog's bowl or opening the refrigerator door. Instrumental or operant conditioning occur when a response is given off at a greater frequency or rate following its association with a reinforcing stimuli or reward. For instance, a rat could be conditioned to expect a food pellet each time the rat presses on a small lever which releases the food pellet, but the rat soon learns it has control over the pace of the ability which it can press the lever and receive a food pellet.

**Confederate.** In research, confederate usually refers to a fellow researcher whether or not he or she is known to research subjects as such.

**Confirmation Bias.** The idea that humans deliberately seek out information from situations or their environment that confirms their already existing notions.

**Conflict.** There are five types of social interaction: exchange, collaboration, competition, conflict, and coercion. Whereas competition of groups has as its reward achieving the goal. Conflict between groups has as the defeat of the opposition as the reward.

**Conflict (approach/theory).** One of the major theoretical perspectives in sociology: emphasizes the importance of unequal power and conflict in society.
- For example: Theorists who are proponents of Marx's work believe that inequality exists between the workers and the owners of the means of productions—industry, financial holdings including companies and corporations, whereas those that support Weber's theory of inequality see the conflict as being between classes and the associated status and power that goes with those classes.

**Conflict Theory and Deviance.** The view that the rich and powerful elite, through their use of power and control resulting from their enormous share of a country's wealth, work to make laws that favor them and maintain the status quo and keep the lower classes in a disadvantaged state that benefits the upper class by their dependence on the former for low-paying jobs.

**Conformity.** When someone goes along with the norms of a group simply for the sake of not wishing to deviate from the group's norms, they are said to be conforming. Conformity is also associated with prejudice in that people may be prejudice because of their desire to **conform to group norms and beliefs.**

**Conformists.** In Merton's strain theory, conformists are those people who want cultural goals (e.g., a nice home, nice car, money in the bank, success in general) and use approved institutionalized means (e.g., hard work, going to college) to achieve those goals. See also, Merton's Strain Theory.

**Cohesiveness.** Refers to the shared bonds between group members.

**Collective Behavior.** Any behavior that results from interactions with others rather than pre-existing norms. For instance, riots and social movements.

**Conjugal Family.** More often than not this term is used synonymously with nuclear family. The relationship is more centered around the legal bonds between husband, wife, and their kids and to a lesser degree blood kin.

**Consensus.** Agreement on an issue by members of a group.

**Conspicuous Consumption.** While simple consumption can be thought of as the consumption of those material goods necessary for survival, conspicuous consumption refers to the consumption of material goods at a rate significantly higher than what is necessary for survival. For instance, class status is highly associated with conspicuous consumption—in other words, people consume more than they need to maintain the perception of their class status.

**Consumerism.** The use of material goods and services to make one happy. Also referred to as consumer culture.

**Conspicuous Consumption.** The consumption of goods and services not thought to be essential to survival and are often performed for the purpose of displaying status and prestige.

**Constitutionalism.** A feature of the American system of government whereby power resides in a written constitution.

**Constitutional Monarchy.** Though a monarchy, the monarch him or herself is more of a figurehead with the real control of government in the hands of elected legislators who do the actual governing. Queen Elizabreth II and Prince Phillip (right).

**Consummation.** The final stage in Freud's theory of the id, ego, and superego in that the actor obtains the object and satisfies the impulse to obtain the object.

**Contact Hypothesis.** There are a number of theories that try to explain why people are prejudice. One such theory is Gordon Allport's Theory of Contact. In it Allport uses previous research that shows people are more likely to be prejudice towards a group of people with whom they have little contact and know only stereotypes about the group. Allport therefore believed that if two opposing groups could be brought together on an open playing field, so that they get to interact with one another, and therefore see through the stereotypes, prejudice might be lessened. This was the government's whole premise behind bussing school children from one school to another—to bring kids of different social and class backgrounds together on a level playing field. While there is some research that finds supports for bussing as a reducer of prejudice, there is not much. Too often school kids would stay in cliques with other people like themselves and the opportunity to reduce prejudice greatly reduced.

**Contagion Theory.** Similar to the idea of anonymity, Gustave Le Bon (right) suggested that the larger the crowd, and the more anonymous they feel, the more likely they can be influenced by radical speech and actions of crowd leaders. Anonymity theory suggests that in large groups when we feel anonymous we are more likely to do or say things we not otherwise do.

**Content Analysis.** A research method used to describe and analyze the media in general. For instance, content analysis has been used to study cartoon violence. Researchers would watch children's cartoons and count acts of violence (as previously qualified before the research began). Based on that research, and similar research on other types of TV programming, researchers concluded that children's TV cartoons have the greatest amount of violence in all TV programming. The aforementioned research is important because many psychological and sociological theories suggest that humans learn violence by watching others and therefore children are being taught violence as normative when viewing cartoons.

**Context of Socialization.** Refers to the setting within which socialization occurs. Also known as an agent of socialization. There are six major agents of socialization: the family, peers, education, media, religion, and military. See, agents of socialization.

**Contingency Model of Leadership.** A theory developed by Fred Fiedler (1963)(right), which suggests there is no one best style of leadership, but instead the most effective leadership style is based on the situation.

**Control Group.** In experimental research, there is a control group and at least one experimental group. The control group's actions or features are held constant without change, whereas the experimental group is exposed to some change. If there is a difference between the control group and the experimental group on the variable being measured, researchers can then conclude that exposing the experimental group to some condition or factor did change some aspect of them that makes them statistically distinct from the control group.

- For example: One hundred undergraduate students voluntarily participate in a study on empathy. The research question is: can empathy be learned? Fifty of the undergraduate students complete a survey measuring their empathy level. We will call them our control group. The second group of 50 students are brought into a room, given a 30-minute lecture on the roots and causes of genocide, and then shown a 30-minute documentary of the Nazi extermination camps during WWII. Only after hearing the lecture and seeing the video do we administer the empathy survey to this second group of students who we have designated the experimental group. After analyzing our survey results and comparing the scores of the two groups, we find the empathy scores to be higher for the second group than the first. In other words, we could make the argument that inducing feelings of empathy during the lecture and movie did in fact change the empathy levels of experimental group—thus theoretically verifying our theory that empathy can be learned. There are certainly other scientific ways of answering our research question, but the above represents one.

**Controlling** (for). "Controlling for…." means to hold a variable constant…taking it out of the equation for the time being when so that the effects of an independent variable or experimental variable may be tested. See above, Control Group.

- For instance, marijuana is associated with crime as is heroin, crack, cocaine, meth, etc. But if we control for possession (i.e., that it is illegal to possess marijuana in most states), we would now find that there is no association between marijuana and crime…unlike heroin, crack, cocaine, and meth which are still associated with crime. Why? Think how the effects of the aforementioned drugs might cause someone to commit crime. Research is very clear that people are more likely to commit crime when under the effects of heroin, crack, cocaine, and meth, but not when they are under the effects of marijuana.

**Convergence Theory.** A theory suggesting that modernizing nations come to resemble one another over time. In collective behavior, a theory suggesting that certain crowds attract particular types of people, who may behave irrationally.

**Conversation of Gestures.** A component of George Herbert Mead's theory of Mind, Self, and Society suggests that there are mindless gestures that are given during a social interaction—often times they serve as an indication that one is listening to another as the other speaks. Nodding as the other person speaks would be an example.

**Cooley, C.** Charles Cooley (1864 – 1929) was a prominent sociologist who developed the concept called the looking glass self (i.e., essentially a mirror). Cooley's concept of the looking glass self suggests that people develop their self-image (i.e., the self) from social interactions and feedback from others. Cooley identified three steps involved in the process he conceptualized as the looking glass self in his book Human Nature and the

Social Order (1902): (1) the imagination of our appearance to others, (2) the imagination of his judgement of that appearance, and (3) some sort of self-feeling, such as pride or mortification.

**Cooperation.** There are five types of social interaction: exchange, collaboration, competition, conflict, and coercion. In this type of social interaction people work together and cooperate to achieve a common goal or secure specific resources.

**Cooptation.** There are several meanings for cooptation. First, inviting people to join an organization at the leadership level so that their opposition to the survival of the organization is nullified. Second, a minority group taking a derogatory term used against them and then using it on themselves. "Mick" is a derogatory word referring to Irish Americans. Irish Americans have coopted the word by using it when speaking to friends and relatives who are also Irish American—"Ah, you ol' Mick."

**Core Nations.** Wealthy nations that have dominant capitalist economies and which control and exploit poorer nations.

**Corporal Punishment** (of children). Corporal punishment refers to the act of punishing a child with the use of physical force. Examples of this kind of punishment includes spanking, slapping, hitting the child with a belt, switch, paddle, or any other material object. There is no evidence to suggest that corporal punishment of children leads to improved behavior on the part of the child when compared to the use of non-physical methods of punishment (e.g., time-out, talking it out with the child, shame).

**Corrective Face-Work.** Ways we try to "save face" after we have potentially damaged the impression others have of us. For instance, if a man thinks it's important that his friends see him as non-violent, he might use the following excuse: "You would have hit him too if he had said that about your girlfriend!" Corrective face-work is done to repair the potential damage to one's impression.

**Correlation.** A statistical tool used to assess the relationship between variables. For instance, as years of post-high school education increases, income increases. A correlation does not necessarily imply cause—simply that

## BENEFITS & COSTS ANALYSIS
*Excerpt: Ford Inter Office Memo, September 18, 1973*

### BENEFITS

| | | |
|---|---|---|
| 180 burn deaths | $200,000 per death | $36,000,000 |
| 180 serious burn injuries | $67,000 per injury | $12,060,000 |
| 2,100 burned vehicles | $700 per vehicle | $1,470,000 |
| | | **$49.5 Million** |

### COSTS

| | | |
|---|---|---|
| 11,000,000 cars | $11 per car | $121,000,000 |
| 1,500,000 light trucks | $11 per truck | $16,500,000 |
| | | **$137.5 Million** |

a relationship exists between the two variables. See, variables.

**Cost.** Relating to Homan's social exchange theory, a cost is something incurred by one actor resulting from a social exchange—for instance, boredom, anger, forgone alternative opportunities. See, Homans' Social Exchange Theory.

**Cost-Benefit Analysis.** The process of making business decisions based on whether the benefits outweigh the costs. It is a rational process and generally makes good sense for an organization. However, sometimes the potential cost can put consumers at risk.

For example, Ford Motor Company began manufacturing the Ford Pinto in 1971 as a competitor to the VW bug. In 1977, it came to public attention that the Pinto had a serious design flaw that could lead to the deaths of occupants resulting from a rear-end  collision at relatively slow speed. In a governmental investigation, a memo was discovered in which Ford had done a cost-benefit analysis on the issue—in other words, what is it to

recall and fix the vehicle or not fix the vehicle and pay out on wrongful death lawsuits. Ford estimated it would be almost $87 million dollars cheaper to pay out on wrongful death lawsuits rather than to fix the vehicle. In short, Ford put a price on human life.

**Counterculture.** Every culture has a dominant culture and most have subcultures depending on the criteria. A counter culture is in direct opposition to the dominant culture in terms of its norms and values.

**Counterfactual Thinking.** The belief that people consciously or unconsciously review life events in a way other than the way they really happened. See also, rosy retrospection.

**Courtship.** Compared to dating, courtship is a more serious phase in a couple's relationship. Generally, the courtship phase precedes engagement or marriage, or if marriage is not being considered, the courtship phase may precede the couple's agreement to commit to a long-term relationship.

**Creationism.** A fundamentalist belief that all things in heaven and earth were made by God in six days and that the earth is six thousand years old.

**Credential(ism).** A movement that requires more credentials in the workplace in a competitive and more highly technical work world.

**Crime.** A deviant behavior prohibited by law and therefore carries sanctions that will be imposed.

**Criminology.** The scientific study of crime.

**Criminal Justice System.** The criminal justice system is an important social control mechanism. Where there are informal social control mechanisms like socialization, being ostracized, and religion in place, the criminal justice system constitutes a formal mechanism for social control. Using official policies and law as its foundation, the criminal justice system administers formal sanctions to punish and deter violations as well as rehabilitate the offender.

**Crude Birth Rate.** The total number of live births per 1,000 persons.

**Crude Death Rate.** The number of deaths per 1,000 persons.

**Crude divorce rate.** Measures the number of divorces per 1,000 of the total population.

**Cult.** A cult is a small religious community that represents a major departure from the beliefs of its parent religion. Usually cults have a charismatic leader, a doctrine that represents a radical shift in thought from the parent religion, is viewed as deviant, and usually requires members to alter their lives.

**Cult of Domesticity.** True manhood depended on how well a male provided for family; true womanhood depended on how well a woman performed duties of wife, mother, and homemaker.

**Cult of Youth.** Society's obsession with all things related to the appearance of youthfulness.

**Cultural Capital.** Those components of culture that are valued and can be used to acquire material goods, substantial income, and high standard of living.

**Cultural Change.** The process by which norms and values of a culture are transformed over a period of time.

**Cultural Deprivation.** The absence of cultural components--norms, attitudes, and values.

**Cultural Determinism.** The belief that culture shapes who and what we are and in turn people within that culture shape society in an ever-changing and evolving process.

**Cultural Diffusion.** Cultural elements of one culture or society are spread to other cultures and societies generally by more advanced societies. These cultural elements are diffused throughout the world with the aid of technological advancements in communication and transportation. One would be the adoption of the Christmas tree—a standard expectation at Christmas started in the 15th century Germany and spread to other Christian cultures over hundreds of years.

**Cultural diversity.** The differences found among cultures.

**Cultural Division of Labor.** A person's position in the labor force is determined by cultural factors—e.g., ethnicity, race, gender, sexual orientation.

**Cultural Imposition.** One dominant or controlling culture forces its beliefs and practices on the lesser culture.

**Cultural Lag.** When one part of society makes a change in a cultural practice but others do not, a cultural lag exists. A timely example would be the decriminalization of marijuana in a number of states.

**Cultural Materialism.** The theory that physical and economic components that build a particular society influence the organization of that society including values and norms.

**Cultural Pluralism.** The coexistence of different subcultures within a society. See also, pluralism.

**Cultural Relativism.** A belief system that counters ethnocentrism. Cultural relativism suggests that other cultures should be studied and evaluated within the context of their own culture and not by the culture of the researcher or evaluator.

**Cultural Revolution.** A sudden social change leads to the displacement of old cultural elements with new ones. The Chinese cultural revolution of 1966 serves as a good example.

**Cultural Transmission.** See, socialization process.

**Cultural Universals.** Cultural elements that are and have been found in every culture down through time. Examples of cultural universals include marriage and the family, language, funeral rites, humor, art, hygiene, deviance, and prohibitions against incest.

**Culture.** The values, norms, and material goods a people use and produce as they share in their distinct identity.

**Culture Industry.** The view that the media serves to make culture a more important element in the economy.

**Culture Lag.** Cultural lag refers to the gap in time that occurs between a technological change or innovation and the related changes in culture.

**Culture of Consumption.** A way of life characterized by mass consumption; values, beliefs, norms revolve around consumption patterns where individuals are defined by what they own.

**Culture of Honor.** A Southern tradition associated with manners and maintaining honor.

**Culture of Poverty.** The belief that the poor are distinctly different from the dominant culture in their values and norms. The belief comes from an oversimplification of Oscar Lewis' (right) book titled, "The Culture of Poverty." Lewis did find that often his subjects, poor Puerto Ricans living in New York City, did have different values and norms, but that those values were temporal and a function of survival. When many of his subjects were able to leave the inner city, the majority replaced their survival norms with the more acceptable norms of the dominant culture.

**Culture Shock.** Alienation or disorientation resulting from extreme or rapid social change within a given culture.

**Cyberbullying.** Bullying that occurs over electronic communications is called cyberbullying. Examples include social media sites, e-mail, text messages, and chat sites. While bullying often is physical in nature, the intent of cyberbullies is more about psychologically harming the victim by spreading rumors, sending mean or menacing e-mail, threatening, posting embarrassing photos or videos. Almost half of all teenagers with access to electronic communications media report being a victim of cyberbullying in the previous year. Children who are victims of cyberbullying are at greater risk of suicide. See also, Bullying.

**Cyberterrorism.** Terrorism using electronic means to disrupt electronic communications and computer networks.

**Dahrendorf, Ralf.** Ralf Dahrendorf (1929 – 2009) (below) was a German sociologist known for his work on class conflict. Rejecting Marx's two class system as too simplistic, Dahrendorf believed there was a two-class system like Marx. What Marx labeled the "haves" Dahrendorf called the "obey" class, and what Marx labeled as the "have-nots," he called the "command" class. Dahrendorf believed that  societies were composed of three groups that were divided into obey and command classes, and those were: (1) quasi groups, (2) interest groups, and (3) conflict groups. Dahrendorf's theory attempts to incorporate aspects of structural functionalism with conflict theory as he explained a far more complex system of social inequality and change.

**Data.** Information that is measured in some systematic way.

**Dating.** Today, because dating does not necessarily lead to courtship, and because it serves transient purposes of companionship, participating in social activities where it is expected for people to bring their dates, and sexual experimentation, it is no longer customary to equate dating and courtship.

**Dating Violence.** A type of interpersonal violence, dating violence refers to one dating partner abusing the other. Examples include controlling behavior on the part of the abuser, tracking behavior (e.g., following, checking cell phone records), and/or physical, emotional, or sexual abuse. See also, domestic abuse.

**Death rate.** The number of deaths per 1000 people per year.

**De Tocqueville, Alexis.** De Tocqueville (1805–1859) was a French philosopher, political activist, and writer. He is known for his seminal work, *Democracy in America*. De Tocqueville was impressed and fascinated at how democracy had resulted in improved social conditions and standard of living for the American people. Believing that democracy in America was balancing liberty and equality, especially when dealing with emerging economic market  forces, he wrote positively of the American democratic experience and used his work to influence the French political process.

**Debriefing.** The process by which research participants are presented with the facts of the research after the research participant has finished his or her involvement.

**Debunking.** To expose the truth about a situation; to dispute a stated claim; to investigate the real intentions or motivations of someone.

**Deception.** A violation of ethical codes of conduct in scientific research. Some limited exceptions are made for this particular safeguard in medical research, but it is rare.

**Deduction.** A research term referring to the process of explaining some phenomenon. Deduction is going from the general to the specific. Deductive reasoning is a top-down approach to scientific discovery. If you think of it as a pyramid, at the top of our pyramid would be the theory we have formed about some phenomena we have observed. Below theory on that pyramid would be one or several hypotheses we wish to test—hypotheses are testable statements. Next down on our pyramid would be specific observations related to the hypothesis that would allow us to test our hypothesis. If after testing our hypothesis the data seem to support our hypotheses by default those supported hypotheses will allow us to confirm or reject our theory.

**De Facto Segregation.** When racial, ethnic and cultural groups are segregated from mainstream society, though that society has laws making segregation illegal. Examples would include housing and cemeteries.

**Deferred gratification.** The willingness to put off the satisfaction of present desires in order for a greater gain in the future.

**Definition of the Situation.** If people define situations as real (i.e., the social construction of reality), then those definitions have real consequences.

**Defining the Situation.** With the use of symbols and cultural elements humans construct reality.

- For instance, if someone were to attend a wedding and see a woman sobbing into a handkerchief, most of us would define the situation by analyzing the woman's tears within that context or situation—i.e., they are tears of joy. On the other hand, what if after that same wedding we were to pass a woman sobbing into a handkerchief while sitting on park bench all by herself? Would we interpret her tears in the same way we interpreted the tears of the woman attending the wedding with us? Almost certainly not. The context is different. So, we construct a different reality: the woman is crying because she is sad or depressed. In both of the aforementioned examples, we have constructed our realities. Doing so is useful because it helps us think about ourselves within that situation. Do we offer the woman crying at the wedding to put her in touch with a therapist? Do we offer the woman crying on the park bench a Kleenex and then go our merry way? What if you are at work or school and you hear what sounds like gunshots? Your construction of reality, how you interpret the sounds within the context of your workplace or school, may be crucial to your survival. But like all things social, your interpretations and construction of reality may be wrong. The woman crying at the wedding may be doing so because it is her former boyfriend that is getting married. The woman crying on the park bench might be doing so because she just won the lottery for 10 million dollars. Or what sounds like gunfire may be a truck backfiring—though in the latter case, and in the world in which we currently live, it would probably be more functional to assume the worse and then carefully decide the reality of the situation.

**Dehumanization.** The process of psychologically reducing one people by another to sub-human. Often used during war. For instance, during the Vietnam war we referred to the North Vietnamese as "gooks," and during the war with Iraq we referred to them as "towel heads."

**Deindividuation.** When people interact with others in a large group, they may experience a loss of self-awareness--in other words, no longer see themselves as an individual accountable for his or her actions. This is a common occurrence during riots.

**Deindustrialization.** When industrial societies move from industry as the main economic mainstay to information technology or service economies.

**De jure segregation**. The separation of races by law.

**Deligitimization.** Closely related to dehumanization, this is the process whereby outgroups are categorized into very specific extreme groups that are often seen as a threat to the dominant group. Seeing members of the outgroup as sub-human leads their being seen as illegitimate group and therefore a target of extreme discrimination and violence.

**Democracy.** Politically power rests directly in the hands of the people and is exercised by voting. By this definition the US is not a democracy but rather a representative-democracy—we appoint politicians to represent us in the political process. Greece is often hailed as the creator of democracy, but because so many Greeks were excluded from the process (e.g., woman, young men, the poor, slaves) it would probably be fairer to say that ancient Greece created the forerunner of democracy.

**Democratic State.** There are three characteristics of the democratic state: (1) people participate in government, (2) there is an election of officials, and (3) there is a multi-party system. The People's Republic of China considers itself a democratic state, but because it doesn't have a multi-party system, it fails to live up to the characteristics of a democratic state.

**Demography.** The study of a population and population changes. Demographics refer to some important fact-based characteristics of a group being studied.

**Demographics.** Characteristics that describe the group being studied. For example, sex, age, educational level, and race/ethnicity are demographics.

**Denomination.** In countries that do not have ecclesia (i.e., churches affiliated with the state like the Church of England) a denomination is a large religious body, independent from the state, with a formal doctrine that dictates beliefs and practices. Well-known denominations today would include Baptists, Southern Baptists, Methodists, Episcopalians, and Roman Catholics.

**Dependence.** Homans' social exchange theory posits that people are rational creatures and will only enter into, or remain in, social relationships in which they experience a profit. Specifically, Homans suggests that only when the reward of a social interaction exceeds a cost, and therefore results in a net gain or profit, will that interaction be repeated or maintained. Dependence suggests that when an actor perceives the cost exceeds the reward of that interaction, the actor will not repeat or maintain that social interaction. Dependence can be used to study why abused women remain in abusive interpersonal relationships. There are a number of reasons abused women stay in an abusive relationship such as the abuser makes them think they will never be able to find anyone else if they leave him, they still love the abuser, they have no job skills, they fear for their lives, and other reasons. The research suggests that at some point most abused women will leave an abusive relationship. Dependence suggests that at some point abused women perceive the cost of staying in the relationship as exceeding the reward(s) of staying in the relationship and they will attempt to leave—though it takes most abused women an average of six to seven times of trying to leave before they are successful.

**Dependency Theory.** A perspective that suggests that first world industrialized nations use the cheap labor found in third world countries and their local resources to fuel economic growth in those industrialized nations. The theory also suggests that industrialized nations suppress industrial development in those third world nations as that would then put them in a position to compete with industrialized nations.

**Dependent Variable.** There are two types of variables: independent and dependent. The independent variable is manipulated, so depending on how the independent variable is manipulated, the dependent variable is literally dependent on what is done to the independent variable and so it will vary.

- Example 1: Let's say we wanted to measure the effects of education on income. We will identify education as the independent variable. Allowing respondents the choice of selecting how many years of education they had, we are manipulating the variable of education. Consequently, we would expect that the number of years of education would result in the dependent variable being effected—i.e., income going up or down based on the number of years of education completed.
- Example 2. We could also study the effects of study time on grades or more generally, G.P.A. (grade point average). If we identified study time as the independent variable, the variable would vary according to how many hours in given amount of time students reported studying. Again, this would be how we manipulated the independent variable. Next, we would identify G.P.A. as the dependent variable—i.e., as the independent variable varied according to how many hours students reported studying, we would expect the dependent variable to change accordingly. Generally, the more hours spent studying, the higher student G.P.A.s.

**Depletion.** Human use of resources past the point they are sustainable, or in the case of renewable resources, it is past the point they are replaceable.

**Deregulation.** Governmental freeing of corporations from laws that are in place to protect consumers, workers, and the environment.

**Descriptive Study.** A research method used to describe some phenomena, whereas explanatory studies attempt to explain why and how the phenomenon occurs. For instance, a descriptive study might describe the behavior of people who have been indoctrinated into a cult or radicalized into a terrorist group. An explanatory study might explain the process cults and terrorist groups use to indoctrinate those new adherents.

**Deskilling.** Historically, craftsmen had advanced skills in their craft and this led to greater income when compared to the masses. Over time, the process of breaking down individual tasks in the manufacturing process led to a reduced need for highly skilled craftsmen. This process of deskilling has led to workers concentrating on more singular and less complex tasks and this has resulted in a reduction in wages.

**Detailed Division of Labor.** Associated with greater productivity, it is the breakdown of individual tasks into simple tasks that are repeated over and over again. One worker to one task. See also, McDonaldization of society.

**Deterrence Theory.** A belief that if the criminal justice system were to bring accused criminals to court quickly, and that those convicted would be punished with certainty and severity, the process would effectively serve as a deterrent to others.

**Deviance.** Deviance in its simplest definition is non-conformity. Violations of social standards. Deviance varies by time and culture. Émile Durkheim (1858 – 1917) believed that both deviance and crime were not only inevitable, but also desirable because it can bring about positive change. Tolerance of deviance is associated with more highly developed democratic societies and is generally healthy for those societies as it stimulates innovation and positive change. Biological theories of deviance focus on biological factors as being responsible for crime and deviant behavior. However, there is no evidence to support a biological theory of crime. Previous research reported an association between body size in males and greater likelihood of juvenile delinquency, but this has largely been discredited. Likewise, Cesare Lombroso (1835 – 1909), the father of modern criminology, reported that criminals had physical characteristics that made them distinct from non-criminals, but this too was discredited long ago. Psychological theories of deviance and crime focus on the personality. It is thought that certain personality traits might be associated with crime, but this too is subject for debate. The only agreed upon psychological aspect that is associated with crime are some types of mental illness—in particular, untreated schizophrenia.

**Deviant Attachment Theory.** A theory that attempts to explain deviance, and possibly crime, by suggesting that people who attach themselves to deviant groups will likely conform to those deviant norms. For instance, people who associate themselves with gangs will adopt the norms practiced by the gang if they want to belong to that gang. Likewise, there is research that reports children who are raised in a home where one or both parents have been incarcerated have a significantly higher risk of being incarcerated as an adult.

**Deviant Identity.** When someone sees themselves as deviant.

**Deviant Sub-Culture.** A sub-culture where its members see themselves as having a different system of norms and values.

**Dialectic.** The process of discovering facts by breaking down the reasoning of another person's arguments into contradictions.

**Dictatorship.** The domination of government by a supreme leader who exercises complete control of the citizenry. Recent examples include Joseph Stalin of the Soviet Union, Adolf Hitler of Nazi Germany, and Saddam Hussein of Iraq.

**Diaspora.** The expulsion of a people from its native land often leads to the scattering of those people around a much larger geographical area. For example, the expulsion of Jews from Judea and Africans from Africa because of the slave trade.

**Differential Association Theory.** A theory associated with deviance. Differential association advocates that people can learn deviant norms by being part of a deviant group. For example, gangs, cults, and offending families.

**Diffusion.** New ideas and technologies have the potential to be adopted by more than one culture.

**Diffusion of Responsibility.** A social psychological concept used to explain why sometimes people are less likely to take responsibility for their actions or inactions when other people are present.

**Direct Democracy.** As an ideal type, the purest form of a democratic government in which all citizens participate in all governmental functions and decisions.

**Disability.** A physical, mental or emotional impairment that results in someone being denied active and equal engagement in social life.

**Discrimination.** Often people who are targets of prejudice by others are also victims of discrimination by those same people. Prejudice is the attitude whereas discrimination is the act. Treating people differentially based on some characteristic(s): race, ethnicity, sex, sexual orientation, religion, height, weight, or age.

**Disintegration.** The fragmentation of society when various groups break away from mainstream society and this weakens the cohesiveness of the society as a whole.

**Disorganization.** A chaotic and unstable social system having devolved from one of order and stability.

**Distributive Justice (exchange theory).** A proposition of exchange theory that states actors engaged in an exchange expect each other's costs and rewards to be equal.

**Division of Labor.** The way specific duties or tasks are organized or delegated in the workplace, at home, in the community or overall society. For example, in the workplace, tasks are usually assigned to specific jobs (and each job has its own job description). CEOs head the company and are responsible to shareholders; supervisors are responsible for supervising the quantity and quality of the work by their subordinates; assembly line workers are responsible for a specific task as the product moves down the assembly line.

**Division of Household Tasks.** In the home, the assignment of household tasks will be influenced by many factors—e.g., educational level of both spouses, income of both spouses, upbringing, and hours spent in the workplace. Women continue to perform a disproportionate amount of the household tasks when compared to their husbands. Generally, women who come from traditional homes, and lack higher education and a career, perform more of the household tasks than do women who come from more progressive homes, have a college degree, and a career.

**Divorce.** The termination of a legally recognized marriage by a court or other legal entity. See also, annulment.

**Domestic Abuse.** Any abusive behavior (e.g., physical, psychological, verbal, or neglect) targeting children, spouses, or the elderly. Explanations for domestic abuse include dependency, intra-individual dynamics, social learning (intergenerational transmission of violence), isolation, and stress. See also, child neglect, child sexual abuse, child pornography, (forced) child prostitution, and interpersonal violence. See also, interpersonal violence.

**Discrimination.** An act resulting from prejudice toward members of a particular group.

**Domestic partnership.** The legal recognition of an unwed couple whose purpose is to grant the same rights to unwed couples that is enjoyed by those legally married.

**Dominant Status.** Sometimes referred to as Master Status. A status is a position or positions we occupy based on an invisible hierarchy of power and privilege. Examples of statuses include: sex, employment status, marital status, age, parental status, class, race, ethnicity, and educational status. We occupy several statuses at the same time. Of those statuses we hold, there is one that overshadows the others—one status that society considers most important. It is the society that determines which status is most important when defining a person and not the status that the individual thinks is most important. For instance, while a mother might consider her status as a mother most important, society says being a woman is likely her master or dominant status. Why? The single most likely reason for discrimination in the labor force is gender. The next most likely reason for discrimination in the labor force is race/ethnicity. So, society essentially says to women you are less important than men (i.e., your status position is lower than that of a man), and it says to African-Americans and Hispanics you are less important than White or Asians (i.e., your status position is lower than that of a White or Asian person).

**Door-in-the-Face Technique.** A social psychological concept that explains a common tactic used by salespeople. The idea is to request a large compliance, which is immediately rejected, and then follow that up with a smaller compliance request, which is more likely accepted--and the real intent of the salesperson.

**Double Hermeneutic.** The belief that researchers may unintentionally have an impact on the social group being studied and thereby alter in some way the group they are studying. Star Trek fans can equate this warning to the "Prime Directive."

**Double Standard.** To say there is a standard for something is to say there is a single method of treatment for people in the pursuit of some goal—everyone has to do the same thing(s) in order to reach that goal. A double standard implies there is a standard for one group of people and a separate and distinct standard for another group people even though both are pursuing the same goal(s). While the term can be used in many contexts, within sociology it is generally meant to refer to sex and race/ethnicity. For instance, to say there is a double standard for men and women means that there is a standard for men and a separate standard for women. Today, only about 15% of all high-level CEO positions are held by women. Generally, women have to work harder to get ahead in the workplace than men, and often times have to give up having a family to compete in "a man's world."

**Dramaturgical Analysis.** An approach to social situations developed by Erving Goffman in his book, "The Presentation of Self in Everyday Life." In Erving Goffman's Dramaturgical Perspective, he believed that people worked to manage the impression others have of them using something called "face-work." He believed that like actors, sometimes we are on-stage (also known as front-stage) and sometimes we are off-stage (also known as backstage). When people are on-stage, they work to manage their impression—an activity that constrains them like an actor on stage playing a part. And like an actor, we manage our on-stage impression differently as the people we are around varies. Further, Goffman believed that we worked to manage the impression others have us with the knowledge of cultural values, norms, and beliefs guiding us. In his dramaturgical model, the goal of the self (i.e., the actor) is to succeed in managing that impression (i.e., one's performance on-stage) to the "audience."

**Dual-career marriage.** A marriage where both partners are employed outside of the home.

**Du Bois, W.E.B.** American sociologist who fought institutionalized racism by urging African-Americans to political action. He was instrumental in leading African-Americans away from the Republican Party, which they had supported since the time of Abraham Lincoln, because of their lack of support of African-American rights and causes. He was also the first African-American to earn a doctorate from Harvard. W.E.B. Du Bois also founded the N.A.A.C.P. (National Association for the Advancement of Colored People) in 1909.

**Dual-Career Families.** In 1950s America, the normal pattern was for the husband to work and the wife remain home to do housework and tend to the children. The 1950s were an economic boon in the U.S. By the 1960s, the economy began to slide and has continued to do so since. The result is that a new pattern emerged: that of both spouses working outside of the home for pay.

**Dual-Career Responsibilities.** The research is very clear on this point: women who are in the paid labor force along with their husbands still do a disproportionate amount of housework and childcare in addition their participation in the paid labor force. Also, because women are socially seen as caregivers and providers, they are more often likely to take time away from the paid labor force when compared to men. See also, division of household tasks.

**Dual Labor Market.** The belief that the paid labor force is divided into fields in which men dominate and fields that women dominate and that those fields in which women dominate are generally lower paid.

**Durkheim, Émile.** Émile Durkheim (1858 – 1917)(right) was a French sociologist and considered the father of sociology. Durkheim wanted sociology to be completely distinct from other disciplines like philosophy and psychology and have its own methods for discovering social facts. Émile Durkheim (right) was the first to use scientific principles in the relatively new science of sociology. He used those principles to study people and groups. Durkheim was the first to advocate that the social world affected people's behaviors. While Durkheim's greatest legacy is that of the father of separate science known as sociology, he is also known for his influence on structural functionalism.

**Durkheim (on religion).** While Durkheim is widely known for his research on anomie, he also studied religion. Durkheim reported that all religions had some major commonalities. Those commonalities are:

- Beliefs. Beliefs explain the unexplainable within a person's ability to understand.

- The sacred and the profane. The profane are those things that we strive to rise above in life; things that are an ordinary part of life like greed, selfishness, and adultery. The sacred are those things which inspire us with a sense of awe. For example, the cross or crucifix, holy beads, and holy water.

- Rituals and ceremonies. Routinized behaviors that reinforce the faith and cohesiveness of the believers. For instance, chants, prayer, and genuflecting.

- Moral communities. Communities of people who share the same beliefs and values.

- Personal experience. Durkheim believed that members of a religion experience a personal relationship with the particular deity and that relationship can give purpose and meaning to people's lives.

**Dyad.** Two people interacting (communicating). For instance, of three possible dyads female/female, female/male, and male/male, research has found that female/female dyads rate the highest in quality of communication while male/male rates the lowest.

**Dynamic Density.** Refers to population density and the amount of social interaction within the group. As social ties and connections grow, people of a group become dense. The group transforms from mechanical solidarity to organic solidarity. Density of human interactions refers to the degree people in a group know each other. In other words, if one person was friends with six people, and all six of those friends were friends with each other, we would say the friendship network is dense.

**Dysfunction.** Used in systems theory (functionalism) to refer to anything that disrupts the normal interdependence of the parts of a system and threatens the system meeting its goal(s).

**Ecclesia.** A church formally allied with the state. For instance, the Church of England, Islam in many Middle Eastern countries.

**Ecological View.** A view of culture that includes those elements in the environment that affect culture. Those elements would include their food supply, access to water, weather conditions, and threats from competing cultures.

**Ecology.** The scientific study of interactions among organisms and their environment. Today, because organisms are now recognized to include man, it is an interdisciplinary field that includes biology, environmental science, and sociology.

**Economic Capital.** The total economic resources an actor controls and has at his or her disposal.

**Economic Core (countries).** The economic core relating to the world economy refers to large multinational companies that are highly profitable and that profit comes from exploiting the labor and resources of third-world countries. Periphery countries depend on the core countries though the wealth is not shared equally.

**Economic Growth.** An increase in the amount of goods and services produced and sold.

**Economic Institution.** As a type of social institution, an economic institution is made up of organizations that produce goods and services that are then distributed to and consumed by society. The repetitive interactions between these components is what makes it an institution.

**Economic Periphery.** Small companies that exist on the fringes of the economy and because of that more likely to come in and out of the economic sector as some fail and other small businesses start up.

**Economic Surplus.** When goods and services produced exceed those required to live.

**Economy.** How the production of goods and services are organized within a given society.

**Ecosystem.** The merging of a system (e.g., humans, organisms in general) with the environment in which it exists.

**Education.** Historically, tribes and clans adhered to an oral tradition of storytelling to communicate knowledge and the history of the people from one generation to the next. With the invention of the printing press, the oral tradition largely gave way to the written word as a way to pass down that knowledge and history. Today, along with the written word, that knowledge and history is passed down formally through the educational system. In addition to passing down knowledge and the history of the culture, the formal educational process passes down the cultures, values, and behaviors as one of the agents of socialization. See also, socialization.

**Efficiency.** The most effective method of achieving some goal.

**Egalitarian Marriage.** A marriage in which both husband and wife are considered equal in decision-making. Note that an egalitarian marriage does not imply an equal division of labor between husband and wife.

**Egalitarian System.** A socio-economic system where all the members essentially have the same in the way of possessions. A system where resources are distributed equally between members. Marx believed that hunting and gathering societies were egalitarian, because being nomadic societies, possessions were a liability when it was time for the society to move to a new location.

**Ego.** Sigmund Freud, the father of modern psychiatry, developed a theory of personality that included three components: the id, ego, and superego. The id is that part of us that, even though its actions are unconscious, drives us to pleasure and self-gratification. Very often the id also represents impulsivity. The superego is that part of us that has resulted from socialization and therefore often counters the id because of its need to adhere to morals or principles. The ego on the other hand is that point in between the two extremes of the id and superego. It serves to "mediate" between the id and superego using its primary principle: rationality.

**Egoistic Helping.** The theory that, like Homan's Social Exchange Theory, posits that man is rational. As such, man does nothing without the expectation of being rewarded somehow. That reward may be financial or materialistic, but it may also be as simple of thinking of him or herself as a "good person," or a "good friend."

**Egoistic Suicide.** Émile Durkheim believed that some people suffered from what he termed anomie. Anomie is a condition where people feel cut off, isolated, unclear of what is expected of them, without purpose or meaning, and disconnected from the larger group to which they belong. Durkheim believed that anomie could lead to suicide under the aforementioned conditions.

**Elder Abuse.** Acts of abuse (i.e., psychological, emotional, physical, or neglect) directed at the elderly usually by adult children.

**Elderly Dependency Ratio.** The ratio of elderly who are not participating in the paid labor force to those people who are. The principle is that those in the workforce, primarily aged 18 to 64, are largely supporting those who are not in the paid workforce (retired people aged 65 and over).

**Elite.** Those people in a given society who dominate because of their wealth and power.

**Elitist.** A belief held by members of a society that a class of people have a disproportionate amount of power, wealth, and prestige and use that power to maintain the status quo.

**Emancipation Proclamation.** During the height of the American Civil War, in January of 1863, U.S. President Abraham Lincoln issued the Emancipation Proclamation. The proclamation stated, "that all persons held as slaves," within those states in rebellion with the United States, "are, and henceforward shall be free." Lincoln likely had several objects in mind: (1) it raised the moral plain of the  war which effectively kept Britain and France out of the war, (2) eyeing the end of the war, Lincoln didn't want the former Confederate states to re-enter the Union with slavery intact, and (3) Lincoln detested in every sense and form the institution of slavery.

**Emigration.** Movement of people out of their native country. Whereas immigration is the movement of people to their new country.

**Emotion Work.** Inappropriate and spontaneous reactions in specific situations can negatively affect us. Therefore, we work to manage our emotions so that those reactions are more appropriate for the situation. Within relationships, significant others work to manage how they react emotionally to the actions of their partner. In the workplace people work to manage their reactions to actions of others and especially their superiors. Failing to do so may have severe consequences for relationships and in employment.

**Empathy.** The ability to see things from another's perspective. To put oneself "in another person's shoes."

**Empirical.** Facts obtained through scientific research.

**Empirical Perspectives.** Ways of looking at only the facts (data).

**Empiricism.** The belief that knowledge comes from observation and experience.

**Encounters.** Erving Goffman called focused interactions an encounter. Encounters are separated by what he called markers or brackets. Brackets help us understand when a focused interaction begins and ends. For instance, can you think of ways that you would acknowledge the beginning of an interaction and the end of an interaction that you might have with friends? One of the most common ways is to simply say, "hello." Likewise, one of the most common ways to end the interaction is to say, "bye." These would-be examples of brackets.

There could be many examples of brackets-not everyone says hello and goodbye, but usually people have something symbolic either words or actions that signal to the other parties engaged in the interaction that it is starting or ending. Along with this are the subtle nonverbal cues that we may give people we are interacting with that we wish to end the interaction. A good example might be, "I've got to go study for an exam." It would be expected that the person in which you are engaged in conversation would understand that you need to end the interaction which then would leave it up to them in most situations to say something to the effect of, "Okay, I'll talk to you later." But sometimes that doesn't happen. Sometimes you could be engaged in interaction with a friend that doesn't pick up on those subtle cues—those friends from hell—the ones that are hard to get away from. Have you ever been in that kind of situation? How have you handled it?

Another good example would be that of telemarketers. When a telemarketer calls, and because we don't know who it is when we answer the phone, we say hello-we have given our bracket so that both parties know that the interaction is about to begin. But as they begin to pitch what they have to sell, and you are not interested, you look for ways to end the interaction, but they will not make that easy for you because they have a script to help them deal with those and other kinds of similar situations. So, if you say I'm not interested, which should be a bracket ending the conversation, instead leads to a scripted response. We are taught from early childhood that it would be improper to simply walk away from someone who was speaking, but telemarketers often force us to do just that—to hang up the phone even though they are still talking. So, this latter situation would be a good example of differences in brackets-saying "hello" was a bracket indicating the beginning of the interaction, but hanging up the phone while the telemarketer was still talking served as a bracket saying that the interaction was over.

**Endogamy.** Restriction of mate selection to people within same group.

**Enlightenment.** Philosophical movement in the 17th and 18th centuries that believed the answer to social issues could be found in the logic of reasoning and science.

**Entrepreneur.** A person who starts a business.

**Entropy.** A gradual decline of a system into disorder. A term usually associated with structural functionalism and systems theory.

**Environment.** In reference to sociology, the social systems that surround an individual.

**Epidemiology.** The study of health and disease.

**Equal Rights Amendment.** Equal Rights Amendment was authored by Alice Paul (1885 – 1977), who headed the National Women's Party, in 1923. The Equal Rights Amendment would have guaranteed equal rights to women. In order to be amended to the US Constitution, 2/3s of U.S. states had to ratify the proposed amendment. Without this amendment, there exists nothing in the U.S. Constitution or Bill of Rights that guarantees the same rights for women as they do for men.

There are three sections to the proposed amendment. They are:

- Section 1. Equality of rights under the law shall not be denied or abridged by the United States or by any state on account of sex.
- Section 2. The Congress shall have the power to enforce, by appropriate legislation, the provisions of this article.
- Section 3. This amendment shall take effect two years after the date of ratification.

**Equality.** The equal division of something. For instance, the equal division of household tasks.

**Equity.** The perception of fairness even in the presence of inequality.

**Equity Theory.** A theory that states that man ultimately seeks equity in social exchanges with others. If they feel that the exchange is not equitable for them, they will seek to change the exchange so that it provides a more equitable outcome for them. See also, Homan's Social Exchange Theory and in particular his distributive justice proposition.

**Equilibrium.** The goal of every system is homeostasis—i.e., the individual parts of a system remain stable and constant so that the system continues to survive. Equilibrium is another term used to describe this desired state in systems theory or structural functionalist theory.

**Equilibrium Theory.** The idea that when change occurs in one part of society, it causes other social institutions to adapt and change as well.

**Estate System.** In an estate system of stratification, there were three classes: the nobility, the clergy, and commoners. The nobility owned the land and commoners worked the land.

**Ethnic Group.** The common cultural heritage of a group which includes their shared ancestry, language, religion, rituals, and food. The U.S. Census Bureau formally recognizes six ethnic categories: Caucasian, African American, Native American and Alaskan Native American, Native Hawaiian and Pacific Islanders. Note: People often use the term ethnicity and race interchangeably, but they are very distinct terms. Ethnicity refers to shared cultural elements and race refers to biological distinctions—though the term *race* is very contentious.

**Ethnic Identity.** When a person's ethnic group is a dominant influence on their life and they largely interact with others of the same ethnic group.

**Ethnocentrism.** The belief that one's own culture is superior to all others and that belief is used to judge other cultures independently of their unique cultural elements. The converse of ethnocentrism is cultural relativism which advocates objectivity when evaluating other cultures and to do so with their particular cultural elements in mind.

**Ethnography.** A type of qualitative research (as opposed to a quantitative research). Ethnography involves the study of unique cultural elements of a given culture and the lives of its individual people.

**Ethnomethodology.** The study of a people by investigating the routine lives of the people within that culture with special emphasis on how they communicate with one another.

**Eugenics.** A movement in the early 20th century that advocated a healthy gene pool could only be created by selecting out of that gene pool people who were genetically inferior. For instance, in 1927, U.S. Supreme Court judge, Oliver Wendell Holmes Jr. (right), who supported eugenics, wrote the following majority opinion in a case brought before the court on Virginia's right to force sterilization on the "feeble-minded:"

> "We have seen more than once that the public welfare may call upon the best citizens for their lives. It would be strange if it could not call upon those who already sap the strength of the State for these lesser sacrifices, often not felt to be such by those concerned, to prevent our being swamped with incompetence. It is better for all the world, if instead of waiting to execute degenerate offspring for crime, or to let them starve for their imbecility, society can prevent those who are manifestly unfit from continuing their kind. The principle that sustains compulsory [sterilization] is broad enough to cover cutting the Fallopian tubes."

After the decision, Holmes concluded his argument by stating: "Three generations of imbeciles are enough."

**Eurocentrism.** A belief that European culture is superior to all other world cultures.

**Euthanasia.** Essentially, physician-assisted suicide of those determined to be terminally ill with less than six months to live.

**Evaluation Research.** A type of social research that collects data to assess the effectiveness of specific social programs. On a smaller scale, evaluation research that focuses on specific organizations and whether they are meeting their stated goals is often referred to as needs assessment.

**Evangelicalism.** Evangelicals consider themselves reborn in the eyes Jesus Christ through a process of formal conversion (which entails repentance for past behaviors). Evangelicals preach the word of Jesus Christ as a way to salvation and adhere to a fundamentalist view of the Bible.

**Evolution.** The scientific theory that all organisms adapt to their physical environment in order to survive as a species. Adaptation is seen as a random process with specific adaptations aiding in the survival of the species, and thus the species evolves and continues to survive, or in the case where a species either does not adapt to environmental changes or those adaptations are functional for survival in a particular environment, die off as does the species.

**Evolutionary Psychology.** The perspective that the more adaptive man's psychological traits have been to changes in the environment down through time, the more likely those traits will be passed down biologically from generation to generation.

**Evolutionary Theories.** Evolutionary theories attempt to apply the theories of biological evolution to societies. They tend to advocate that societal change is the result of the society's adaptation to changes in the environment and in so doing become more advanced can adaptive.

**Exchange.** There are four types of social interaction: exchange, collaboration, competition, and coercion. An exchange interaction suggests that people exchange things, tangible items like material goods, or intangibles like affection and emotional support.

**Exchange Network.** A social network made up actors who have a wide range of resources they can exchange with others who value those resources. Exchange relationships within these networks are often interdependent so that there is a single exchange network structure.

**Exchange Theory.** Also known as Homan's Social Exchange Theory. A theory that attempts to explain the basis for man's interaction with others. George Homans took the economic model of exchange and advocated its application to the study of human social interactions. Exchange theory suggests that we are in a constant state of social exchanges with others. Based on economic theory, exchange theory suggests that when we profit from a social exchange, we will most likely repeat it, but if we don't profit, we will most likely not repeat the exchange. Homans' social exchange theory has 13 propositions that attempt to explain exchange relationships. See also, Homans, George.

**Exogamy.** A social more that requires people to find mates outside of certain groups—such as their own family.

**Expectations States Theory.** A theory that proposes status hierarchies are formed during social interactions. It suggests that different levels of status are assigned to people in these groups largely dependent on someone's ability to successfully complete the task or goal at hand. Closely related to this line of thinking is what is referred to as "status carryover." Status carryover suggests that statuses carry over between situations even if having status in one area is not necessarily useful in another. For instance, studies have found that frequently people with high occupational prestige (e.g., doctors, CEOs, bankers) are more often selected as jury foremen even if their occupational status is marginal or even irrelevant to the jury's task.

**Experiment.** Experiments usually occur in laboratories or carefully controlled environments where the independent variable can be manipulated. The manipulation of the independent variable ideally will lead to a corresponding change in the dependent variable. If there is a change in the dependent variable, and in the predicted direction, researchers would consider the result supporting the stated hypothesis.

**Experimental Group.** Generally, there are two research groups: a control group, in which conditions are not varied, and an experimental group in which conditions are changed or manipulated. The experimental group is exposed to the manipulation of the independent variable.

**Experimental Methods.** See, experiments.

**Explanatory Study.** Explanatory studies are used to study how or why things happen. For instance, when studying crime rates, research has repeatedly found that crime rates are higher in inner city areas than in the suburbs. Our explanatory study would be interested in discovering the reason(s) for this fact.

**Explicit Attitude.** Explicit attitudes are attitudes that we are consciously aware of and guide our behaviors.

**Explicit Cognition.** The belief that unconscious thoughts and attitudes influence our behavior though we are consciously unaware of them.

**Exploitation.** Karl Marx believed that in a capitalist system the "haves" earned and controlled the majority of economic rewards, but that the "have-nots" receive just enough to survive even though they actually perform more labor than does the "haves." In other words, the "haves" exploit the labor of the "have-nots" to their advantage and reap most of the rewards associated with that labor.

**Expressions of Intimacy.** Nonverbal communication, in other words, what we communicate with symbols, includes expressions of intimacy or lack thereof. In many countries, certain forms of words are used that convey intimacy--like the distinction between "Usted" and "tu" in Spanish. Here in the US we make no such distinction—which therefore deprives us of information that could be used to help us interpret an interaction.

Another example of expressions of intimacy would involve words that are generally reserved for special others. The words "honey," "darling," "sweetie," are typically reserved for intimate others. If we as strangers hear one person use one of those words to the person he/she is with, we will interpret the word to indicate that they have some kind of intimate relationship.

Finally, touching is symbolic in that it is often interpreted by others who view the act even without knowing the people involved.

**Expressive.** Expressive or affective are roles assigned to people by society based on their sex. Woman, culturally seen as nurturers, are expected to be more emotional than men.

**Expressive Leader.** There are generally five types of leadership styles: (1) instrumental, (2) expressive, (3) authoritarian, (4) democratic, and (5) laissez-faire. An expressive leader focuses on maintaining the effectiveness of the group by encouraging and supporting group cohesion. Expressive leaders tend to use expressive work to maintain friendly and warm interactions with their subordinates. This kind of leadership style tends to earn the trust and effect of subordinates. Research suggests that highly effective leaders need to have both expressive and instrumental leadership styles.

**Expressive Roles.** Roles that involve taking care of personal relationships; usually taught to women; nurturing, emotionally attentive, passive, etc.

**Expropriation.** Often associated with the conflict perspective, it is when land, wealth, property, or labor is confiscated from someone.

**Extended Family.** A nuclear family consists of a father, mother, and their children. An extended family, which is the normative type of family in many parts of the world, is multi-generational and consists of a father, mother, their children, their elderly parents, and other relatives living under the same roof.

**External Attribution.** People attribute other's behaviors to situational factors. For instance, Asians are stereotypically thought to be the best students *because they are Asian.*

**Eye Contact.** Eye contact is also very important in our culture. We expect others to maintain eye contact with us when we are engaged in focused interactions. For instance, Sue who was friends with Sally, is curious whether or not there is something between Sally and her boyfriend, so she asks Sally, "Sally, did you sleep with my boyfriend?" Where should Sally's eyes be as she responds to Sue's question? imagine Sally staring at the ceiling as she says to Sue, "No, of course not."

**Experimenter Demand.** A type of bias within research in which subjects or respondents do or say what they think the experimenter wants them to do or say rather than how they actually feel or act normally.

**Expressions of Status.** Expressions of status involve the interpretation of symbolic symbols. There are two types of expressions of status: (1) status using words as symbols (e.g., referring to people using words that are associated with status in our culture like "Sir" and "Dr.), and (2) paralinguistic status. Paralinguistic status refers to research findings that report people who are typically regarded as having higher status within organizations or society as a whole tend to talk longer, louder, more frequently, and are more likely to interrupt when working in mixed status task groups. When status is given to people in situations where that status should be irrelevant, it is called status carry-over. For instance, research on jury studies has found that jury foremen generally have higher status in society (e.g., doctor, CEO), but jurors accept that higher status as relevant to the job of jury foreman when in fact it is irrelevant.

**Expulsion.** The forced physical removal of a minority group from territory claimed by the dominant group. Examples include the expulsion of Native Americans to reservations, Jews from Europe during the Inquisition and then again after the Nazis took over Germany politically.

**Face.** Parts of different identities that we get attached to and feel that we must defend.

**Face-work.** Erving Goffman is considered to be the father of what is called impression management. Simply put Goffman believed that we worked to manage the impression of others have us when we're in public and we use symbols to do it. That work to manage our impressions is called face-work and it is done to protect our self-esteem. See also, impression management.

**Fads.** Cultural changes that lead to new behaviors or attitudes that become widely adopted. Generally, these attitudes and behaviors only last a short time before giving way to newer fads. Examples would include: platform shoes and bell-bottom pants for men, Beanie Babies, boom boxes, Nintendo, thongs for women, and selfies.

**False Consensus Effect.** The belief that people assume that their attitudes, opinions and behaviors are normal and typical of other's attitudes, opinions, and behaviors, too.

**False Consciousness.** In Karl Marx's perspective on the evolution of social stratification, he believed that at some point all societies would be reduced to only two classes: the bourgeoisie, or the owners of the means of production and sometimes referred to as the "haves," and the proletariat, those who worked for the bourgeoisie and sometimes referred to as the "have-nots."

Over time as the bourgeoisie continued to oppress proletariat, they would realize they were part of a mistreated group—in other words, a shift in conscious would make them realize it wasn't just them as individuals who were being mistreated. This realization that the proletariat were all part of one large mistreated group led to what Marx referred to as "class consciousness." Only after the development of a class consciousness would the proletariat unite and rebel—either by demanding change or outright revolution. But, Marx went on to write, one thing could interfere with class consciousness resulting in change or revolution, and that was the development of what Marx called "false consciousness." False consciousness literally means the acceptance by a mistreated group of an ideology that was contrary to their best interest. While Marx believed that there were a number of ideologies that could lead to the development of false consciousness, he identified religion as one of those ideologies. Marx believed religion was used by those with power (i.e., the haves) to keep the have-nots in place as second-class citizens. Marx is quoted as saying religion was the "opium of the people." His meaning was that religion, like opium, kept people docile and passive.

What most people don't know that when he wrote about religion being the opium of the people, he was referring to the American institution of slavery. Marx saw Christianity being forced on slaves by their masters because Christian values would keep the slaves in place. For instance, there are references to slavery throughout the Bible, and in those passages, there appear admonitions to slave owners to treat their slaves with compassion and passages that command slaves to obey their masters. The Bible justified the second-class position of slaves. Further, the Bible clearly states that murder is wrong, keeping slaves from rising in the middle of the night and killing their masters, and that stealing is a sin, which kept a slave from running away because technically they were the "property" of their masters.

Marx's work can be applied to many situations we see today where people are divided into classes—one group holding power, and the other group as being dominated the other. For instance, race, wealthy versus the poor, men versus women. See also, Equal Rights Amendment.

**False Uniqueness Effect.** The belief that the attitudes and opinions they have, and the behaviors they exhibit, are unique and therefore they are different and uncommon.

**Family.** There is no definitive agreed upon definition of "family." Because of dramatic cultural changes in the past two decades, previous definitions simply do not apply. Previous definitions included that members were related by blood, but this would exclude adopted or foster children and technically stepchildren as well. Previous definitions would also state that families live together, form an economic unit, are between a man and a woman, and they have sexual relations (between the adult partners). But these too are a problem. But these latter characteristics are problematic, too. There are a number of reasons that families may not live together for some period of time—for instance, one or both partners are in the military, one partner must travel extensively for their job, and commuter couples (i.e., couples that because of their careers must maintain separate residences). While it is assumed that families will form an economic unit, many couples do not share financial resources—they may have completely separate bank accounts or have a shared account but additionally each has their own separate accounts. Likewise, while in the past marriage was between a man and a woman, the recent Supreme Court decision to make illegal state laws prohibiting same-sex marriage has changed that previous characteristic of the "family." Finally, it should not be assumed that all marital partners have sex. There are a number of reasons couples may not have sex. Further, with age comes a redefinition of what "sex" is—younger people tend to think of sex as being oral or vaginal intercourse, but research has found that definition changes for some elderly— e.g., hand-holding, sitting close together, kissing, and cuddling.

**Family of Orientation.** The family into which one is born.

**Family of Procreation.** The family one begins.

**Fashion.** To "be in fashion" suggests that people are dressing or adorning themselves in the current approved style. Consequently, fashion changes constantly and can be associated with trends and fads.

**Fatalistic Suicide.** In social situations where people feel they have no control over their life because the socioeconomic system regulates that life so completely, they may feel depressed, alienated, and hopeless that they are more likely to commit suicide.

**Female Infanticide.** The systematic killing of female infants at or around birth.

**Femininity.** Sex refers to the biological distinctions between males and females. Gender refers to the roles and behaviors of males and females that are culturally defined. Femininity refers to specific behaviors and roles culturally assigned to women, but in reality, are demonstrated by both males and females to varying degrees. For instance, in our culture men are not expected to cry, but some men do—some while at the funeral of a loved one and others while watching a sad movie. Women are culturally defined as nurturers, yet two of the top ten snipers in history were women.

**Feminism.** Attitudes and behaviors with the goal of furthering political and social rights for women.

**Feminism of Poverty.** Studies have found that poverty is increasing among women at a disproportionate rate.

**Fertility.** The birth-rate in a particular society.

**Feudalism.** A system of stratification where nobles are provided land by a monarch in exchange for their loyalty and service if needed to fight off an enemy. The land is worked by peasants or what is known as vassals.

**Field Research.** Quantitative research usually uses surveys to collect data which is then turned into numbers so that it be used to test hypotheses. Qualitative research is more interested in the quality of the data and not testing hypotheses by analyzing numerical data. Field research is a qualitative method used to collect data from people in their normal setting because it is interested in studying them in their daily lives. Sociologists will often employ what is called participant observation as a type of field research. While there a number of different types of participant observation, below are there of the most common types:

- Passive participation in which the researcher only observes and records.
- Active participation is where the researcher fully joins the group being studied. The advantage to this type of participant observation is that the researcher has an in-depth understanding of the group being studied. The disadvantage is that the researcher may identify with the group so completely that they lose objectivity.
- Complete participation is when a member of a group to be studied is enlisted to provide data on the group's behavior. Again, the risk is a lack of objectivity.

**First World.** Generally, sociologists, political scientists, and economists referred to three types of societies: first world, second world, and third world. Of the three types of societies, only third world is still used as a label. Western industrialized countries are labeled as first world countries, former states of the Soviet Union were labeled as second world countries, while developing nations are still labeled as third world countries.

**Flextime.** The ability of workers to negotiate their work schedule.

**Focus Groups.** A form of qualitative research consists of a group of people who are brought together to provide information about some issue in question. Focus groups can be used to elicit opinions, values, beliefs, and commercial products.

**Focused Interactions.** A focused interaction is when two or more people are directly attending to what others are saying. So, let's say that you are now at that same party and you see a friend. You walk up to the friend and begin to talk to them-you are now engaged in a focused interaction-your attention is now on the conversation occurring between you and your friend.

**Folkways.** Folkways are norms that when violated carry either no or slight sanctions. For instance, what if you went to a wedding and at the proper time you turned to watch the bride walk down the aisle, but as you did so, you noticed that she was wearing a bright red dress. Do you call the police? Do you stop being her friend? No. There are likely no sanctions that you will impose even though it is a violation of norms. The norm says that women should wear a white dress to their wedding. There could be sanctions though minimal. For instance, what if you turn to the person next to you and snickered or made a face. In some sense those are sanctions, but as you can see they are not severe. Other folkway violations might include picking your nose, passing gas, belching, wearing a hat indoors, or eating with your fingers. Here in the US you're supposed to use utensils for eating with a few exceptions—sandwiches, French fries, pizza, etc., but in other parts of the world such exceptions may not be made.

**Foot-in-the-Door Technique.** The social psychological belief that if someone wants another to perform a large compliance, they start off asking for small compliances from the other, with each requested compliance, and that compliance is given, eventually that person will agree to a large compliance-- though they might not have done so if someone had started off by asking for that large compliance. The other term for this process is called successive approximations.

**Fordism.** The system of assembly line technology developed by Henry Ford.

**Formal Organizations.** Organizations with a clear hierarchy of authority, written rules and regulations, and clear goals or objectives.

**Formal Sanction.** Sanctions are punishments for social norms that are violated. There are three types of norms: folkways, mores, and taboos. While there may be no or slight sanctions for the violation of a folkway, there will always be sanctions for the violation of a more or a taboo. In the case of a more, the sanctions may be informal or formal (if a law is broken), and in the case of a taboo, because violating a taboo threatens the survival of a culture, sanctions are always administered and severely administered (e.g., the death penalty).

**Foucault, M.** Michel Foucault (1926 – 1984) (right) was a philosopher and sociologist. Foucault is known for his work on the use of power and knowledge by social institutions as a form of social control. During Hitler's reign in Germany (1933 – 1945), the German state defined some people as "undesirables" or mentally deficient. In $18^{th}$ century England, the poor and homeless were often labeled in the same way. Philip Stokes, in his book "Philosophy: 100 Essential Thinkers," wrote the following about Foucault's legacy: "The theme that underlies all Foucault's work is the relationship between power and knowledge, and how the former is used to control and define the latter. What authorities claim as 'scientific knowledge' are really just means of social control. Foucault shows how, for instance, in the eighteenth century 'madness' was used to categorize and stigmatize not just the mentally ill but the poor, the sick, the homeless and, indeed, anyone whose expressions of individuality were un-welcome."

**Freud, Sigmund.** Sigmund Freud (1856 – 1939) (right) was a physician, philosopher, and psychiatrist. He is considered to be the father of psychoanalysis and his theories heavily dominated field of psychology, though to a lesser extent today. Freud developed what he referred to as a "science of the mind." Freud's work continues to influence psychology and is used by a significant number of psychiatrists and clinicians in their work with patients.

**Front.** Our entire face that we present to others; the method through which we cue others to the self and identity that we claim.

**Front-Stage (on-stage).** In Erving Goffman's Dramaturgical Perspective, he believed that people worked to manage the impression others have of them using something called "face-work." He believed that like actors, sometimes we are on-stage (also known as front-stage) and sometimes we are off-stage (also known as backstage). When people are on-stage, they work to manage their impression—an activity that constrains them like an actor on stage playing a part. And like an actor, we manage our on-stage impression differently as the people we are around varies. Goffman believed that because on-stage activities were exhausting, people need time in which they can come off-stage where they can relax and recoup. It is while off-stage people can be at ease and think about their performance while on-stage and decide if there is improvement their on-stage self needs to make. See also, backstage or off-stage.

**Frustration.** An emotional state when something interferes with goal-directed activities.

**Frustration-Aggression Hypothesis.** Theory that as people are unable to reach set goals and become frustrated the emotional outlet for that pent-up frustration is anger.

**Functional Approach.** An analytical approach that uses the tenets of systems theory to examine a social system. Systems are composed or interdependent parts that work together to accomplish system goals. Systems exist within a surrounding environment which supplies it with raw resources and to which the system exports a finished product of some type. All systems have boundaries that separate it from the environment and those boundaries can be discerned. Finally, all systems have goals to which they work.

**Functions.** According to structural functionalist theory, behavior or acts have consequences for the group as a whole. There are functions, which may be intended or unintended, and dysfunctions. For instance, the intended or manifest function of the rain dance for Native American tribes is to make it rain, but research reports there is an unintended or latent function of the rain dance—the rain dance increases cohesiveness of the tribe because it brings members together in an important ritual.

**Functions of Law.** The legal system negotiates relationships between social actors; it integrates different social actors.

**Functions of Polity/Government.** Establish goals and social control.
**Functions of the Economy.** The extract raw resources from the environment, convert them into usable goods, and transport those goods and services to the society.

**Fundamental Attribution Error.** (Also known as FAE). An error in reasoning that occurs because people are better able to see external forces affecting their behavior than they are in seeing how those external forces affect the behavior of others. For instance, if John receives an F on a test, he might reason that he got an F because his roommate kept him up all night playing loud music, but if Susan receives an F, and especially if Susan is from an ethnic or minority group, John will most likely attribute her F to a personality deficit--"they're not good students," or "they're lazy."

**Fundamental Innovation.** Technological innovations and emerging social and economic trends that stimulates the development of further innovations and leads to rapid social and economic change.

**Fundamentalism.** Religious fundamentalism strictly adheres to a rigid and literal interpretation of a specific religious text, generally believes in an afterlife of some kind, and has a clear-cut moral code that dictates right from wrong. Fundamentalism can be associated with any religion.

**Game Stage.** Referring to the process of the development of the "self," the game stage is the last stage. The game stage is characterized by the ability to participate in organized games. In this stage, they learn about the importance of playing by the rules, their particular role as a member of a team, and the roles performed by their fellow teammates. The central goal of the game stage is for the child to be able to take on the role of other players at the same time—in other words, to see things from the perspective of the other players. See also, Mead, G. H.

**Garfinkel, Harold.** Harold Garfinkel (1917 – 2011) was an American sociologist who coined the term ethnomethodology. Ethnomethodology is a field that studies the way people come to understand the everyday meanings of their social situations.

**Gang.** An informal group whose members practice deviant and often illegal activities.

**Gemeinschaft.** Ferdinand Tonnies (1855 – 1936) was a German sociologist who proposed there were two types of social groups—Gemeinschaft and Gesellschaft. Gemeinschaft, according to Tonnies, was characterized by small, tight-knit, traditional society that was centered around the community and had close relationships with fellow members of the community. On the other hand, Tonnies characterized **Gesellschaft** as an urban state, individualistic, impersonal, and ties between people were primarily based on self-interest and monetary exchanges. Aside from modern capitalist states, corporations are often used as examples of Gesellschaft.

**Gender.** Socially constructed traits and behaviors that are assigned to people based on their sex.

**Gender Differences.** Differences in the expected behaviors, roles, and attitudes between men and women.

**Genderelect.** A linguistic style that reflects the differences between how men and women communicate.

**Gender Identity.** A person's conception of their self along a continuum of gender ranging from male at one end of the continuum to female at the other end. Traditionally, gender has been limited to the self as either being male or female, but recent and dramatic sociocultural changes have led to a much broader understanding of the complexities of a person's gender identity.

**Gender Inequality.** The differential and unfair treatment of men and women primarily in the workplace. Gender inequality is largely the result of stereotypes.

**Gender Mutilation.** Surgical procedure that involves removing the clitoris and labia in order to control a woman's sexuality.

**Gender-Role Expectations.** Gender norms to which people are expected to follow.

**Gender Schema.** The mental constructs people have about gender and the appropriate roles that should be carried out by people based on their gender.

**Gender Socialization.** Also known as differential socialization. Gender socialization begins at birth. Boys and girls are put on different paths depending on their sex. Research has found that boys are encouraged to play sports while girls are encouraged to play with dolls; parental reactions to the same behaviors are different for boys and girls; boys are most likely praised for their physical abilities while girls are more likely praised for their appearance and scholastics. Research has also found that there is a significant difference, and largely stereotypical portrayal of men and women in the media. When boys and girls step off the path that is assigned them by society, they are often sanctioned. For instance, a little girl who climbs trees may be called a "tomboy" while a little boy that likes to play with dolls may be called a "sissy." Remember, sanctions are designed to punish a behavior and bring the person back into line with social norms.

**Gender Stratification.** Gender stratification is when there is unequal status between men and women and that unequal status affects their power, prestige, and privilege in society.

**Gender-Based Occupational Segregation.** When compared to men, research has found that women are most likely found at the bottom of the paid labor force holding jobs that are generally unskilled and low-paid. The ratio of males to females in the U.S. population is 48/52. All things being equal, we should expect to see that ratio in everything we study. In other words, 52% of the 43 presidencies we have had in the U.S. should have been held by women if all things were equal, but of course, there have been none as of the time this was written. Further, of the top 500 CEO positions in the U.S., 52% should have been held by women, but in actuality it is 4%. Out of 50 state governorships, only five are held by women. Finally, 80% of all clerical workers in the U.S. are female. The message here is clear: all things aren't equal.

**Generalized Other.** As part of the developmental process, people become aware of the attitudes, norms, and values of other members of society.

**Generalization (prejudice).** Generalizations are assumptions that if people

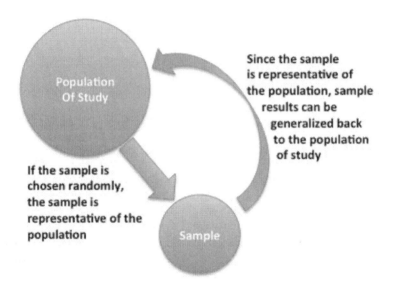

believe something is true of one or several people, it must be true for the entire group.

**Generalization (research).** When random sampling is used to select a smaller sample from that population, the sample should be representative of the population from which the sample was extracted. That allows researchers to generalize their results from the sample to the population of study; in other words, if some specific results are true of the sample, they should also be true of the population.

**Genocide.** The deliberate destruction of a minority group. There are five ways a dominant group can treat minority groups: (1) genocide which is the intentional destruction of a minority group, (2) expulsion which is the driving of the minority group from a geographical area by the dominant group (and which often results in genocide), (3) segregation which is the dominant group's use of the minority group for its labor for there are clear divisions between the dominant and minority group, (4) assimilation which is the dominant group's acceptance of the minority group as long as the minority group accepts the dominant group's values, beliefs, and norms, and (5) pluralism which is where are all groups value each other's unique cultural diversity.

For example, the U.S. government in the 1880s, under President Andrew Jackson, resettled Native Americans from South Carolina to the Oklahoma Territory. Jackson perceived them as a threat to the internal stability of the then U.S. This period of forced expulsion is termed the "trail of tears." It is thought that anywhere from 2,000 to 6,000 Native Americans died as a result of this forced march. Even though expulsion was the expressed governmental intention, the result was genocide.

Likewise, in the 1880s both the U.S. and Canadian governments issued smallpox infected blankets to Native American populations with the intent of killing them off so as to make the remaining population submissive to the will of both the U.S. and Canadian governments. This is another example of genocide.

**Gentrification.** The movement of middle-class and upper-middle-class persons (usually white) into lower-income, sometimes minority urban areas.

**Gesellschaft.** See, Gemeinschaft.

**Ghandi, Mohandas K.** Mohandas Gandhi (1869 – 1948) (right) was the leader of the Indian independence movement. At that time, India was part of the British Empire, and Gandhi was actively in the independence movement. He is the first in recorded history to use nonviolent civil disobedience as a way to deal with oppressive regimes, systems, or laws. His tactic of non-violent civil disobedience worked and Britain formally  granted independence to India in August 1947. India was made up of both significant Hindu and Muslim populations when it became independent from the British Empire. Factions from both religions openly fought each other. The Muslims wanted their own country and many Hindus opposed this. On January 30, 1948 Mohandas Gandhi was assassinated by Hindu extremists who opposed concessions Gandhi was making to Muslims in order to keep peace between the two peoples. Ranked as the second most peaceful person in history, falling only behind Jesus Christ in first place, Gandhi is known today for his non-violence and belief that all men were equal in the eyes of God. Gandhi's tactic of non-violence was used during the American Civil Rights Movement in the 1960s by Martin Luther King, Jr. to rid the South of the institution of segregation. Like Gandhi, King was assassinated for his work and beliefs in April 1968.

**Ghetto.** A geographical section of a city that is primarily occupied by members of a specific racial, religious, or ethnic group who tend to have few if any financial resources; a part of an urban area where the occupants are primarily made up of the underclass.

**Giddens, Anthony.** Anthony Giddens (1938 – present) (right) is a British sociologist known for his holistic view (i.e., you must study the whole of a system and not just the individual parts) of post-industrial societies, reflexivity in which he believes that actors within a system constantly redefine themselves as they react to other actors within the system, and globalization which uses a systems approach in that world events are shaped by local events and in turn local events shape world events.

**Glass Ceiling.** When women with the same qualifications and education as men cannot rise to the same level as do males, this is called the glass ceiling. Essentially, the glass ceiling is gender discrimination. This is in opposition to the glass elevator in which men in primarily female dominated occupations, such as nurses, rise to the top more quickly than do women. Because of the ration between men and women in the U.S., which is for every 48 males there are 52 females, and if all things were equal, 52 percent of all clerical workers in the U.S. would be female, but in reality, it is 80 percent. Further of the top 500 CEO positions in the U.S., 52 percent should have been held by women, but in actuality it is 4 percent.

**Glass Escalator.** Research has found the men working in female dominated occupations tend to be promoted more quickly be paid more.

**Global Culture.** Cultural components that have been spread globally.

**Global Economy.** An economy in which the economic life and health of one nation depends on what happens in other nations.

**Globalization.** The process by which shared cultural elements and consumerism lead to countries and cultures developing closer ties and less distinguishable from one another.

**Global Stratification.** The unequal distribution of resources between nations.

**Goal Attainment.** A component of structural functionalism that suggests that systems must not only define their primary goals, but also achieve them as well if the system is to survive.

**Goal Displacement.** The primary goal of every system is survival. Sometimes systems will set specific goals, and do such a good in meeting those goals, that the goal is met and no longer can serve as a reason for the system to exist. In the fact of having to cease existence as a system, a system may reformulate its goals. The March of Dimes provides a classic example of goal displacement and replacement. Its original goal was to provide funds for research to find a cure for polio. With the creation of a vaccine against polio developed by Jonas Salk, the March of Dimes had met its goal, but in order to survive as a system, it reformulated its goal to its present goal: to provide funds for research to find cures for all childhood diseases.

**Goffman, E.** Erving Goffman (1922 – 1982) was a Canadian sociologist who investigated people's behavior in social settings. In his book *The Presentation of Self in Everyday Life*, Goffman advocated that in their interactions with each other, humans presented themselves like actors performing on stage. Like in a theatre production, people like actors, worked to manage the impressions the audience had of them and they did this using symbols. Goffman wrote that when humans are managing their impression they are on-stage or front-stage, when they are resting and preparing for their next role, they are off-stage or back-stage. See also, dramaturgical approach.

**Government.** The set of people who are engaged in directing the state.

**Group.** A group of people who share some common goals and who interact in the achievement of those goals on a regular basis constitute a group. For instance, a group of student athletes working together to win a competition make up a group, whereas a group of people waiting on a bus make up a congerie and not a group because there is limited interaction and they are not working together to accomplish some shared goal. Generally, groups can be divided into two types—primary and secondary. The characteristics of primary and secondary groups are:

- o Primary group: face-to-face interactions occurring in small groups that are socially intimate in nature and exist to accomplish goals through cooperation. Primary groups are informal in nature.
- o Secondary group: impersonal, formal in nature, and generally lacking social intimacy.

**Group Polarization.** The tendency of group members to develop attitudes towards some phenomenon that is preferred by the majority.

**Groupthink.** When groups fall into the trap of following a few influential group members, disregard dissenting opinions, and generally failing to "think outside of the box," groupthink may occur. Groupthink limits the amount of critical thinking that might otherwise occur within groups.

**Guilds.** Skilled workers who performed a complex task effectively as a result of a lengthy apprenticeship and training. Guilds were common during European medieval times. Trades included within guilds included blacksmiths, shoemakers, weavers, stonemasons, and other similar crafts that required great skill.

**Guttman Scale.** Louis Guttman (1916 – 1987) (right) was an American social psychologist who developed a psychometric measure that rank ordered responses. The idea behind a Guttman scale is that individual items are arranged so when a respondent agrees with a particular scale item by default they also agree with previous lower ranked items. A Bogardus Social Distance scale is a type of Guttman scale. For instance,  assume the following statements make up a scale: (1) I am ok with having someone of a different race live near me, (2) I am willing to talk to someone of a different race, (3) I am willing to live next door to someone of a different race, and (4) I am ok with my son or daughter marrying someone of a different race. If a respondent agrees with item #4, by default they must also agree with the previous three items. Essentially, a Guttman scale is rank ordered from the least extreme condition to the most extreme condition.

**Habermas, Jurgen.** Jurgen Habermas (1929 – present) is a German sociologist known for his work on the public sphere, critical theory, and modernity. Jurgen Habermas is widely considered as the most influential thinker in Germany over the past decade and is seen following in the tradition of German social thought of **Kant, Marx** and **Freud.**

**Habitus.** A lifetime process of socialization where people absorb and embody ideas about history and culture, and reproduce them without a conscious appreciation of how their ideas of reality came to be formed. Term popularized by Pierre Bourdieu (1977).

**Hate Crime.** When criminals specifically target victims because of their race, ethnicity, sexual orientation, age, gender, gender identity, or disability they are committing a hate crime. For example, in 1988 James Byrd was beaten, had his throat slashed, and then while still alive, and was dragged behind a pickup truck with a chain for an estimated 1.5 miles before dying when his body hit a culvert and his head and torso were torn off. An autopsy showed later that he was alive until he hit the culvert. Of his three assailants, all three were White supremacists and Byrd was chosen simply because of his race.

**Hawthorne Effect.** A source of bias within research when subjects of an experiment act differently than they normally would because they know they are being watched or studied.

**Health Maintenance Organization (HMO).** Health care institutions that minimize health care costs to patients by the greater reliance on general practitioners than on medical specialists when treatment is thought to be within the ability of the HMO to provide adequate and reasonable service.

**Heaven's Gate.** Founded by Marshall Applewhite (1931 – 1997) and Bonnie Nettles (1927 – 1985), Heaven's Gate was a religious cult. Members believed that mankind was the result of interbreeding between man and aliens thousands of years earlier and therefore man is descendent from an alien life form. Believing that the earth would soon be "recycled," members believed that an alien mothership, located in the trail of the comet Hale Bopp, was returning to earth to pick up cult members who  were referred to as "children of the Next Level." When the mothership was thought to be at its closest point to earth, cult members were told they needed to "shed" their earthly "vessels" (i.e., to commit suicide) in order to be transported to the "Next Level." After dressing in black track suits and Nike athletic shoes, 38 cult members in addition to Marshall Applewhite committed suicide by taking phenobarbital with vodka and then tying a plastic bag around their heads. The ages of cult members who committed suicide ranged from 26 to 72 years. See also, Cults, and Jim Jones (and the People's Temple).

**Hegel, G.** Georg Hegel (1770 – 1831) was a German philosopher who is the father of what is known as Hegelianism. His ideas of idealism had a huge impact, both negatively and positively, on the works of Karl Marx, Friedrich Engels, and Soren Kierkegaard. Hegel's work even influenced the writings of Carl von Clausewitz—known for his seminal work, *On War*.

**Hegemonic Masculinity.** Most cultures have been scientifically proven to value masculine characteristics and this leads to a culture which puts emphasis on the possession of those characteristics--assertiveness, aggressiveness, competitiveness, and toughness.

**Heider's Balance Theory.** Fritz Heider (1896-1988)(right) was an Austrian psychologist. Heider proposed that we seek balance in our relationships with others and things. For instance, if John likes Susan, Susan is pro-abortion, and John is pro-abortion, then a balanced relationship exists and no cognitive dissonance occurs (see, cognitive

Figure 1. Heider's Balance Theory. The first image represents a balanced relationship while the second image represents an unbalanced relationship.

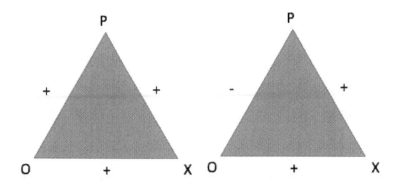

dissonance). On the other hand, if John likes Susan, Susan is pro-abortion, but John is not, the relations are unbalanced which in theory would cause John to experience cognitive dissonance and this dissonance eventually lead to him changing his position on abortion or not like Susan any more. The aforementioned example can be seen in the figures below. In the left figure, the relationships are balanced, but in the right figure, they are not. In the figures below, P is a person, X is a person, and O represents another person or object. So, using our example, P represents John, X represents Susan, whom he likes, O represents pro-abortion attitudes. In the first figure, John approves of abortion, noted by a plus sign, but in the second figure, John disapproves of abortion and this is noted with a negative sign.

**Heterosexual.** A person whose sexual preference is for someone of the opposite sex.

**Heuristics.** Sometimes when people or researchers attempt to solve a problem, they attempt to draw on what they think they know about that particular phenomenon. Heuristics offer a quick but usually imperfect way of dealing with a novel situation or a problem that needs to be solved. Sometimes referred to as mental shortcuts. Stereotyping or profiling others are examples of heuristics in play, as are educated guesses or guesstimates. It is their continued belief that constitutes the danger of heuristics because people may stop looking for other often disconfirming information.

**Hidden Curriculum.** The belief that the educational system provides socialization in areas outside the formal curriculum. For instance, when students are expected to raise their hands in class they are being taught to respect authority.

**Hierarchy.** An authority structure with power and decision-making flowing from top down.

**High Culture.** Valued and used by an elite minority they are artistic and intellectual works thought to be of high quality.

**Higher Education.** Formal education beyond high school. Usually refers to college or university level education.

**High-Trust System.** Workplace occupations where workers are given great autonomy.

**Hindsight Bias.** Also known as the 'I-knew-it-all-along' effect. For a number of reasons, hindsight is a significant defect in memory and judgement because it causes memory distortion. This is hugely important when humans or researchers are influenced by hindsight bias and this leads to flawed understandings and methodological research problems.

**Hinduism.** Hinduism is a polytheistic religion, confined mainly to India and parts of Africa, and principles of Dharma (i.e., correct living).

**Hispanics.** A very general term that refers to people whose primary native language is Spanish. The term provides little in the way of meaning because ethnic diversity is so great; in other words, Hispanics would include Mexicans, Puerto Ricans, Cubans, Central Americans, South Americans, people from some Caribbean islands, and even Spain.

**Historical Materialism.** A theory proposed by Karl Marx in which he suggested that man must produce material goods necessary for life in order to survive and this production must exist from one generation to the next. In order for man to produce these material goods efficiently, they must establish dependable relationships with one another. Marx referred to these as "production relations." He believed that in the process of producing these goods efficiently, man must create a division of labor in which people perform different jobs in that production process. However, Marx stated that those who owned the means of production (i.e., the tools necessary to produce those material goods), profited by the labor of those who did not own the means of production—in other words, they worked for those who owned the means of production.

Marx's clearest formulation of his "materialist conception of history" was in the 1859 Preface In his book, *A Contribution to the Critique of Political Economy* (1859), wrote the following in his preface:

> "In the social production of their existence, men inevitably enter into definite relations, which are independent of their will, namely relations of production appropriate to a given stage in the

development of their material forces of production. The totality of these relations of production constitutes the economic structure of society, the real foundation, on which arises a legal and political superstructure and to which correspond definite forms of consciousness. The mode of production of material life conditions the general process of social, political and intellectual life. It is not the consciousness of men that determines their existence, but their social existence that determines their consciousness. At a certain stage of development, the material productive forces of society come into conflict with the existing relations of production or — this merely expresses the same thing in legal terms — with the property relations within the framework of which they have operated hitherto. From forms of development of the productive forces these relations turn into their fetters. Then begins an era of social revolution. The changes in the economic foundation lead sooner or later to the transformation of the whole immense superstructure. In studying such transformations, it is always necessary to distinguish between the material transformation of the economic conditions of production, which can be determined with the precision of natural science, and the legal, political, religious, artistic or philosophic — in short, ideological forms in which men become conscious of this conflict and fight it out. Just as one does not judge an individual by what he thinks about himself, so one cannot judge such a period of transformation by its consciousness, but, on the contrary, this consciousness must be explained from the contradictions of material life, from the conflict existing between the social forces of production and the relations of production."

**Homans, G.** George Homans (1910 – 1989) took an economic model of exchange and advocated its application to the study of human social interactions. Homans' social exchange theory suggests that we are in a constant state of social exchanges with others. Based on economic theory, exchange theory suggests that when we profit from a social exchange, we will most likely repeat it, but if we don't profit, we will most likely not repeat the exchange.  Homans' social exchange theory has 13 propositions that attempt to explain exchange relationships. See also, Exchange Theory.

**Homogamy.** When people date and/or marry someone from the same social background.

**Homophobia.** Irrational fear and hatred of homosexuals.

**Homosexual.** A person whose sexual preference is for someone of the same sex.

**Horizontal Mobility.** In a class system, movement between equal class positions in a status hierarchy. This is in opposition to vertical mobility where a person's class position on the status hierarchy may move up or down. For instance, a first-generation college student will likely have a higher-class position than that of their parents.

**Hospice.** A health care system that provides institutional or at home care to the terminally ill. Hospice agencies also provide some types of assistance to a patient's family including grief counseling.

**Hostage Syndrome.** Traumatic bonding and attachment of the hostage to the hostage-taker. Related to interpersonal violence (domestic abuse).

**Hostile Aggression.** Generally, hostile aggression is spontaneous and a reaction to a perceived immediate threat.

**Household Tasks.** Unpaid housework by members of the household. Research shows that women perform more household tasks than do men.

**Human-Capital Explanation.** The belief that in the workplace differences in education and experience contribute to wage differentials.

**Human Subjects Committees.** Also known as institutional review boards (IRBs). IRBs are in place at colleges and universities who deal with research issues related to using human subjects in that research. Committees must adhere to government guidelines that serve to protect human participants in research. Specifically, committees are concerned that there be no harm to participants, that participation is voluntary, that participants are not deceived, and that participants are informed if the information provided by them will remain confidential or anonymous. In cases where there may be a need to violate one of the aforementioned principles, primarily in medical research, committees will evaluate whether the potential for good outweighs the risks or violations.

**Hunting and Gathering Societies.** The earliest type of society. Members of hunting and gathering societies were nomadic in that after they had exhausted their food supply they would relocate. Because the society was nomadic, possessions were a liability, therefore there was little if any stratification. See also, Marx, K.

**Hybrid Economy.** When examining economic systems, capitalist (i.e., a free market economy) would lie at one extreme of a continuum and socialism (i.e., a centrally planned economy ran by the state) at the other end, a hybrid economic system would be somewhere in the middle on that continuum as a combination of both systems.

**Hybrid Identities.** People who have multiple ethnic backgrounds and use those identities to create their unique self-identity.

**Hyperinflation.** Massive economic inflation that significantly reduces the buying power of currency.

**Hypothesis.** A tentative statement between two variables. See also, Variables.

**"I."** George Herbert Mead (1863 - 1931) in his theory of the development of the self, defines the "I" as the more impulsive and reactive part of the self. The "I" reacts to the "me." The "me" is that part of the self that understands the norms, beliefs, and attitudes of the society in which they live. It is often referred to as the "generalized other." The "I," aware of the past and those societal norms, beliefs, and attitudes, exists in the now or future of the self. The "me" essentially regulates and influences the "I." See also, generalized other.

**Id.** Sigmund Freud (1856 – 1939) (right) was perhaps the most influential psychiatrist in history. His work continues to influence psychological approaches to treatment and research on the mind and cognition. According to Freud, the id was the unconscious impulsive part of the psyche.

**Idealism.** Idealistic thoughts and goals that guide a person's behavior though they may not be realistic.

**Ideal Type.** A perfect form of some concept or phenomenon. Max Weber referred to an ideal type when discussing the rationality of bureaucratic organizations. In reality, ideal types are not achievable, but instead serve to demonstrate a phenomenon in its purest form; a perfect standard used to measure other lesser forms.

**Ideal Values.** Borrowing from the idea of an "ideal type," an ideal value refers to what people identify is important to them even if their values don't support. For instance, someone might say they are not prejudice toward a particular group, but their behaviors may indicate otherwise.

**Identification Theories.** Theories that suggest through a process of parental modeling, children learn gender roles by copying the same-sex parent.

**Identity.** Social positions and roles that we claim as part of our self.

**Ideology.** Ideas, myths, and doctrines that reflects and supports the belief systems of those who hold a particular ideology.

**Idiosyncrasy Credit.** An explanation as to why some people do not fear deviating from group normative behavior or attitudes.

**Idiosyncratic.** Refers to the idea that people react differently to common situations.

**Illegitimate Opportunity Structures.** Based on work done by researchers Richard Cloward and Lloyd Ohlin, the authors proposed that there are paths to "success" goals: (a) an actor holds a position in both legitimate and illegitimate opportunity structures; (b) the greater availability of illegitimate opportunities is seen as the quickest and most lucrative opportunity; and (c) when the actor realizes his or her legitimate opportunities are minimal and he or she is unable to lower their goals, this results in them exploring non-conformist opportunities.

**Illusory Correlation.** Seeing a relationship between two variables where in reality none exists. For instance, someone may believe that every time they wash their car it rains, therefore, why should they wash their car? But because of selective attention, humans are more likely to remember (selectively attend) those times when it rained after washing their car though in reality it has actually been more often the case that it didn't rain after they washed their car. See also, selective attention.

**Imitation Stage**. According to Mead's theory of socialization, this is when children learn to mimic the behaviors of those around them.

**Immigrant.** An immigrant is someone who leaves their homeland for a new country. This is in opposition to an emigrant who is someone that arrives in their new country.

**Impairment.** A physical, mental, or emotional disability that prevents people from functioning and performing normal tasks.

**Imperialism.** A system where a controlling nation exploit lesser and dependent nations.

**Implicit Attitude.** Implicit attitudes are attitudes that are unconsciously but do influence our decisions and behaviors.

**Implicit Cognition.** The idea that our behavior is often the result of unconscious influences. So, while researchers have found that most Americans say they are not influenced by advertising, research says that we are. That research suggests that we may be consciously aware of about 10 percent of a commercial's message, but as much as 70 percent of that message is worked and reworked in our subconscious brain.

**Implicit Personality Theory.** Refers to the biases and flawed processes humans use when forming initial impressions of other people. Several other theories attempt to explain the process of initial impression formation such as consistency theory and attribution theory.

**Impression Formation.** The initial, but often biased and flawed process by which humans form impressions of others.

**Impressions Given.** As a component of Goffman's dramaturgical perspective, Goffman talks about the importance of first impressions. Because people know that first impressions are important, they consider themselves on-stage and actively work to manage the impressions others have of them with the use of symbols—primarily verbal. Those symbols they give off intentionally, and are interpreted by others, are called impressions given. Goffman goes on to say that because people realize the importance of first impressions they may deliberately use those verbal symbols to deceive others.

**Impressions Given-Off.** As a component of Goffman's dramaturgical perspective, he talks about the importance of first impressions. While impressions given are evoked intentionally, impressions given-off are unintentional. These unintentional symbols may damage the impression someone is trying to give. Generally, impressions given off are not verbal, though they could be in the case of a quivering voice which would be an example of paralanguage, but rather non-verbal symbols such as poor posture, fidgeting, poor eye-contact, inappropriate attire for the situation, or sitting with crossed arms. These aforementioned actions will likely be interpreted negatively depending on the context and are therefore counterproductive.

**Impression Management.** In Erving Goffman's book, the *Presentation of Self in Everyday Society*, he writes about something he calls a dramaturgical perspective. Goffman believes that humans in their interactions with others act like actors on stage. Because people want to be seen positively and view themselves, he believes that like the actor on stage, people work to manage the impression others have of them. They do this by the use of symbols, words, things, and behaviors, which are then, interpreted by those with which they are interacting—in other words, their audience. See also, Goffman, E., dramaturgical perspective, frontstage/on stage, and backstage/off stage.

**Impulse.** According to George Herbert Mead, an impulse is where an actor feels an urge (first state of an act) and responds accordingly to fulfil that urge.

**Income.** Paid monetary wages paid to a worker in exchange for their labor.

**In-Group.** An in-group consists of people who we think are like us in some way, we identify with, and belong. We constantly compare ourselves to those in our in-group to measure some aspect of ourselves. An in-group is in contrast to an out-group which are composed of people we feel are different than us in some significant way. Categorizing people as part of a person's out-group is highly associated with prejudice.

**Incest.** Sexual activity with close family members. Most states forbid the marrying of second cousins or closer.

**Incest Taboo.** Perhaps one of the strongest taboos is the incest taboo. Taboos have the potential to threaten a society's survival. For instance, sexual relations between parents and their children or between siblings. Because they are such a severe threat to a society sanctions are almost always harsh.

**Inclusion.** Actively seeking out, valuing and respecting differences.

**Income.** Generally, how much someone makes from wages, interest, tips, and other revenue sources. However, the term is non-specific because a number of variables come into play—for instance, (1) hourly, weekly, monthly, or annually, (2) net (after taxes) or gross (before taxes), (3) individual or household, and (4) in what currency.

**Indentured Servitude.** A type of slavery where a free person agrees to sell themselves and their labor to another for an agreed upon period of time. This was a common method used by Europeans who wanted to immigrate to America but didn't have the funds to do so on their own.

**Independence.** Freedom. A much-used concept, freedom exists along a continuum: at one end would be where person had absolutely no control over their own life--when to eat, sleep, brush their teeth, have sex, but at the other end, there would be absolutely no restrictions and therefore life would be nothing more than complete and total chaos.

**Independent Variable.** The independent variable is the variable that is manipulated in some way and that manipulation produces a change in the dependent variable; the dependent variable is dependent on what is done to the independent variable. While the independent variable is often referred to as the "cause" and the dependent variable as the "effect," a simple relationship between an independent and dependent variable cannot be said to be causal without other conditions being met. See also, causation.

**Indices.** Indices differ from scales in that an index is simply a composite measure that totals scores of individual survey items; any survey question that is designed so that respondents can only answer "yes" or "no," or "true" or "false," would be examples. For example, let's say we wanted to use an index to measure depression. Depression is a complex psychological concept—too difficult to measure by simply asking respondents if they are depressed. There are a number of characteristics that are indicators of depression. So, below is the index we might construct:

1. I often feel sad.                          YES or NO
2. I don't enjoy doing things like I used to.          YES or NO
3. I often think about the past.                 YES or NO
4. My future looks bleak.                     YES or NO

If a respondent circles YES to all four questions, and each YES answer was worth one point since it indicated depression, our respondent would have a score of 4 out of a possible 4—in other words, we would judge him/her as being highly depressed since the maximum possible score was 4. See also, scale.

**Individualism.** The belief that individuals should be able to master their physical and social world and are accountable for their actions. President Herbert Hoover coined the term "rugged individualism" to refer to the idea that people should not depend on others (e.g., the government) but rather on themselves.

**Induction.** A research term referring to the process of explaining some phenomenon. Induction is going from the specific to the general. Whereas deductive reasoning uses a top-down approach to scientific discovery, think of inductive reasoning using a bottom-up approach—i.e., starting at the bottom of the pyramid. At the very bottom of that pyramid are some observations we have made about some phenomena we wish to study. Our goal is to move up the pyramid by generalizing our observations to more and more situations that ultimately lead to a theory. So, after we collect some initial observations about the phenomena we are interested in studying, we then begin to look for patterns in the data that might allow us to state a hypothesis we can then test. If the data allow us to build a number of hypotheses that our supported, we can then build a theory that attempts to explain the phenomena. See also, deduction.

**Industrialization.** The cultural transition from a primarily agrarian economy to one of manufacturing.

**Industrialized Societies.** Societies that have made the transition from an economy based on agriculture to one based on manufacturing.

**Industrial Revolution.** Social change resulting from technological developments in 18$^{th}$ century England. Those technological changes included

the use of waterpower to

create energy that was then used for manufacturing and then waterpower was largely replaced by power created by steam engines. As a result of these new power sources, industry sprang up primarily in cities, which were not prepared for the massive influx of workers from rural areas. Because urban areas were unable to adequately deal with the influx of these new workers, sanitary conditions were appalling, disease rampant, pollution (primarily from coal smoke) led to all sorts of health problems, and poverty was widespread. Though not a sociologist, the English author Charles Dickens (left) wrote much of his work during this period of human history in which he described the miserable conditions that many English had to endure.

**Infanticide.** The killing of infants usually for population control. Infanticide has been a common cultural practice for the past 2,000 years. The practice continued well into the 19$^{th}$ century in China where infant girls were not valued and often killed by being drowned.

**Infant Mortality Rate.** A statistic used to report the number of infants who die usually during the first year of life per one thousand live births. Though infant mortality rates have decreased dramatically in industrialized societies, as of 2017 the US still has one of the highest infant mortality rates in the industrialized world at 5.82 for every one-thousand live births.

**Informal Sanction.** A sanction is usually a punishment. There are formal and informal sanctions. Formal sanctions may include punishment for violations of the law. Informal sanctions are generally mild in their consequence. See also, folkways.

**Informational Influence.** New information or arguments provided in a social context that changes people's attitudes, beliefs or behavior. Informational influence is considered to have its greatest effect when people are uncertain about reality and therefore look to other members of the group for help in deciding what that reality is.

**Informed Consent.** Permission by a subject or respondent to participate in research once they have been told what the research involves, the potential risks, and the potential harm.

**In-Group.** The group to which we identify and feel as if we "belong."

**In-Group Bias.** The tendency to give more credit or belief to the ideas, beliefs and actions of those people consider part of their in-group than they do to members they see as members of an out-group.

**Initiator.** In Dianne Vaughan's book, *Uncoupling* (1990), Vaughan (right) referred to the marital partner who was most dissatisfied as the initiator because they took steps to end the relationship. She found three common steps initiators took as they planned and moved toward the divorce. First, initiators began to spend more time away from home. Second, initiators encouraged their current  spouse to make new friends and develop outside activities. Third, initiators made new friends—Vaughan referred to these new friends as "transitional friends."

**Inner Control.** A component of control theory, a person's conscience or moral code is believed to deter them from acts of deviance.

**Innovation.** Technological changes that have the potential to dramatically change a culture. For example, microwave ovens, cell phones, and social media.

**Innovators.** In Merton's strain theory, people who accept the institutionalized goals, but reject the institutionalized means of obtaining those goals, are called innovators. Innovators are often identified as criminals.

**Instinct.** A biological predisposition towards some behavior.

**Institution of Science.** Science encompasses many fields. All sciences use the scientific method as the basis for their research and research is necessary to discover facts about our physical and social worlds. Because of this shared use of the scientific method to discover facts, we can speak of a community of scientists who together constitute what is called the institution of science. See also, scientific method.

**Institutionalized.** Social institutions are those aspects of societal life that are determined by repetitive, established, patterned, and predictable interactions. The process of an aspect of societal life becoming an institution is called institutionalization. Social institutions include education, government, family, religion, politics, and the economy.

**Institutionalized Discrimination.** Differential treatment that is so embedded in the everyday workings of social life that it is not easily recognized as discrimination and does not require conscious prejudice or overt discrimination (example: height requirements for military, police and firefighters in the US).

**Institutionalized Racism.** State-sanctioned racism in which minority groups lack the same access to services or opportunities afforded other group members in an organization.

**Institutions.** Social institutions are those aspects of societal life that are determined by repetitive, established, patterned, and predictable interactions. Social institutions include education, government, family, religion, politics, and the economy.

**Instrumental.** Instrumental tasks or roles are those behaviors that involve the solving of problems necessary for the maintenance of interpersonal relationships or the health and well-being of a person. For instance, instrumental tasks associated with later life (also referred to as Activities of Daily Living) include the ability to move without assistance, bath themselves, dress themselves, cook and feed themselves, use the toilet without assistance. When people cannot provide these instrumental tasks for themselves, assistance must be provided or their health and well-being will be jeopardized.

**Instrumental Aggression.** Aggression used to accomplish a goal.

**Instrumental Leader.** There are generally five types of leadership styles: (1) instrumental, (2) expressive, (3) authoritarian, (4) democratic, and (5) laissez-faire. The instrumental leader is one who focuses on goal achievement. Consequently, from the organization's point of view, they are efficient at accomplishing their assigned goals. However, the importance of meeting assigned goals can often be at the expense of good relations with subordinates.

This can result in worker alienation and poor job satisfaction on the part of subordinates.

**Integration.** The third component of Talcott Parson's structural functionalist theory that states a system regulates the individual interdependent parts.

**Intended Symbols.** Also known as expressions given. Those symbols we intentionally provide for interpretation to others. See also, dramaturgical perspective, front stage, back stage, and impression management.

**Interactionism.** A belief that human behavior is the result of the effects of both the person and the situation.

**Interaction Ritual.** A form of interaction where individuals perform acts to show reverence to one another which involves a mutually shared meaning.

**Interactions (social).** There are different types of social interactions. They are: exchange, cooperation, conflict, and coercion. Let's look at each of these individually. When two or more people exchange something—for example, material goods, advice, and affect, it is a type of social interaction. Of all the reasons for social interactions, exchange is by far the most common. People interact with each other because they have things to exchange one of those big tangible or intangible commodities. Next, when two or more people work together to reach some shared goal, that's an example of cooperation. In other words, people feel that they must cooperate to achieve their mutual ends, but by so doing they are interacting. When two or more people compete for the same goal, or reward, or scarce resources, that type of interaction is called conflict. Finally, there is coercion. Coercion is using illegitimate authority to get something from others. If I were to demand that a student get me coffee, and threatened to fail them if they didn't, that would be an example of coercion. So, coercion too, is an example of a type of social interaction.

**Interest Group.** Often referred to as special interest groups, these are groups that work to influence politicians on issues affecting the organizations they represent.

**Intergenerational Mobility.** A vertical change of social status from one generation to the next. We can measure where a person is in terms of their class position and then measure where their parents are in terms of their class position. If there is a difference in class position between them and their parents, then we can say that there is evidence of mobility of class positions.

**Intergroup Anxiety.** Anxiety or fear of negative consequences when someone must interact with members of an outgroup.

**Intermittent Reinforcement.** Also referred to as inconsistent discipline. According to learning theory, when behaviors are rewarded, they are most likely to be repeated. This applies to unwanted behaviors as well. Research has shown that inconsistent discipline can result in the reinforcement of an unwanted behavior as effectively as consistent discipline. One example would be single-parenting and juvenile delinquency. Research has found that juvenile delinquents have a higher chance of having come from single-parent households than in-tact households. While superficially this might suggest that mothers heading these single-parent households make bad mothers, research suggests the real reason has to do with role overload. Because single mothers raising children must take on the responsibilities of both parents, and because they most likely work full time, they often suffer from work overload—too much work and responsibility may lead to physical exhaustion. In other words, a mother might come home one day from work and punish her child for some action, but the next day because they are over-worked and exhausted, fail to punish the child for the same behavior. This inconsistent discipline can have the unwanted effect of rewarding and thereby increasing the behavior.

**Internal Attribution.** Attributions for success or failures that result from a person's belief the loci for those successes or failures are found in their personality traits, attitudes, or abilities.

**Internal Validity.** When investigating a concept, it is when the method of measuring the concept is in fact judged to actually measure that concept.

**Internalization.** To internalize something is to take external social factors (e.g., values, beliefs, expected behaviors or norms) and apply them to oneself. Research on juvenile delinquents suggest that if society labels a child as a juvenile delinquent, they might internalize this label and become that very thing, a juvenile delinquent. See also, labeling theory, and self-fulfilling prophecy.

**Interpersonal Attraction.** Physical or emotional attraction of one person to another.

**Interpersonal Distance.** Interpersonal distance refers to the distance we like to keep others based on their relationship to us. Research suggests that we Americans like to keep strangers at about six feet, friends around four feet depending on the friendship, and then intimate others at around two feet or less. When this distance is violated we may feel threatened and find a way to increase the distance.

Another example would include elevators. There are unwritten rules when we ride an elevator with strangers. When you're riding an elevator with a stranger do you stare at them? Do you sing? Do you talk to yourself? No. The most common behavior while riding on an elevator with a stranger is staring at the control panel with the floor numbers or even staring straight ahead at the doors. If Erving Goffman was still with us he would probably make the argument that we do this so we can pretend our interpersonal space isn't being violated because we are in enclosed environment with a stranger and therefore closer than six feet.

**Interpretive Approach.** Building on symbolic interactionism, a theory that examines how people make sense and interpret, with the use of symbols, their social world.

**Intimacy.** The sharing of inner feelings and emotions with another.

**Intragenerational Mobility.** A vertical change of social status within the same generation. We can measure where a person is in terms of their class position and then measure where they are in terms of class position at some later time in their life. If there is a difference in class position between those two periods, we can say that there is evidence of mobility of class positions.

**Intimate Partner Violence.** Any abusive behavior (e.g., physical, psychological, verbal, or neglect) targeting children, spouses, or the elderly. Explanations for domestic abuse include dependency, intra-individual dynamics, social learning (intergenerational transmission of violence), isolation, and stress. See also child neglect, child sexual, abuse, child pornography, (forced) child prostitution, and domestic abuse.

**Invention.** Generally, some new technology. Often these new technologies can lead to cultural change. For example, social media, the Internet, the automobile, fast food, microwave ovens, cell phones, personal computers.

**Iron Cage.** The argument that once a bureaucracy is in place it is impossible to remove; the irrationalities of bureaucracy: dehumanization and increasing inefficiency.

**Islam.** World's second largest religion, monotheistic, and is centered around the word of God as delivered to the Prophet Muhammad. There are two Islamic sects: Shia and Sunni. Approximately 15% of the world's Muslims are Shia and 85% Sunni. The largest concentration of Shia can be found in Iran and parts of Iraq.

**Islamophobia.** Like any prejudice, it is an irrational fear based on stereotypes and lack of information, but in this case, it is directed at Muslims.

**I.Q.** A person's intelligence quotient is a measure of their fluid and crystallized intelligence. Fluid intelligence refers to how adaptive people are to changes and the speed at which they are able to solve problems. Crystallized intelligence essentially refers to knowledge, which results from experiences and learning. It is generally thought that fluid intelligence peaks in the late 20s and begins a gradual decline throughout the rest of the lifespan. On the other hand, crystallized intelligence is always increasing as people learn and experience their environment. An I.Q. test uses a standardized set of questions designed to measure these two types of intelligence. The use of I.Q. as a meaningful measure has largely fallen out of favor in the past several decades.

**Iron Law of Oligarchy.** Robert Michels (1876 – 1936) (right), in his book *Political Parties* (1911), stated that democratic organizations can become so large and complex that they cannot function efficiently as such and will become oligarchies (i.e., rule by a few).

**Jealousy.** A negative emotion that results when a person with a strong emotional attachment to another feels threatened by a rival.

**Jim Crow Laws.** Laws that required separate but "equal" facilities for African Americans in the American South.

**Jim Jones and the People's Temple.** Jim Jones (1931 – 1978) was an American religious leader who founded the People's Temple in 1955. After moving from Indiana to California, the order had its headquarters in San Francisco. The People's Temple was a cult and Jim Jones was the cult leader. After his paranoia led him to think that the government was stalking him, he moved the organization to Guyana in South America  and founded the People's Temple Agricultural Project in what he named Jonestown. After a number of temple members had written loved ones back home in the U.S. that they wanted to leave, but were being held against their will, Congressman Leo Ryan of California led a fact-finding mission to Jonestown. When Congressman Ryan attempted to leave Jonestown via a nearby airstrip, Jones in a paranoid state, ordered some of his henchman to ambush the congressman and those traveling with him. After news reached Jones that the ambush had been successful and Congressman Ryan and his entourage were dead, Jones ordered a "red alert"—an action that indicated the religious group would soon to be overrun by government forces. Using a loudspeaker, Jones urged his followers to commit suicide by drinking a concoction of Kool-Aid and cyanide; those that refused to do so voluntarily were forced at gunpoint. The mass suicide/murder led to the deaths of 918 members of the religious group.

**Judaism.** One of the smaller world religions, it is monotheistic, and believes that the word of God (i.e., the Torah) was delivered to Moses at Mt. Sinai.

**Just-World Belief.** The belief that all that occurs to people in life is equitable and what they deserve—good or bad.

**Juvenile Delinquency.** "Delinquency" is a term that applies to illegal acts committed by children aged 10 to 18—the term "crime" would be used for the same commission of those illegal acts if the accused was older than 18 years. Juveniles accused of delinquent acts aren't subjected to a trial as are people older than 18 years, they instead go through a process of adjudication and then a disposition (i.e., sentencing). There are two types of juvenile offences: (1) acts that would be considered criminal had an adult committed them, and (2) acts that normally wouldn't be considered criminal if an adult had committed them (e.g., truancy, curfew violation).

**Keynes, John Maynard.** John Maynard Keynes (1883 - 1946) was an English economist and father of what has come to be known as Keynesian economics.

**King, Martin Luther, Jr.** Reverend Dr. Martin Luther King, Jr. (1929 – 1968) was an African-American civil rights leader who adhered to Mahatma Gandhi's principles of non-violence in order to bring about social change. Arrested numerous times in his life for protesting against segregation in the South, and for speaking out in favor civil rights for Africa-Americans, King was assassinated on April 4, 1968 in Memphis, TN. During his lifetime King was awarded the Nobel Peace  Prize, and today he is remembered with a national holiday in the U.S. and more than 700 streets are named after him. One of his lasting legacies was his "I Have a Dream" speech given during his March on Washington for Jobs and Freedom action in March of 1963. Only 17 minutes in length, King stated:

> "I say to you today, my friends, so even though we face the difficulties of today and tomorrow, I still have a dream. It is a dream deeply rooted in the American dream.
>
> I have a dream that one day this nation will rise up and live out the true meaning of its creed: 'We hold these truths to be self-evident: that all men are created equal.'
> I have a dream that one day on the red hills of Georgia the sons of former slaves and the sons of former slave owners will be able to sit down together at the table of brotherhood.
>
> I have a dream that one day even the state of Mississippi, a state sweltering with the heat of injustice, sweltering with the heat of oppression, will be transformed into an oasis of freedom and justice.
>
> I have a dream that my four little children will one day live in a nation where they will not be judged by the color of their skin but by the content of their character.
>
> I have a dream today.

I have a dream that one day, down in Alabama, with its vicious racists, with its governor having his lips dripping with the words of interposition and nullification; one day right there in Alabama, little black boys and black girls will be able to join hands with little white boys and white girls as sisters and brothers.

I have a dream today."

**Kinship.** Relationships based on blood or marriage.

**Label.** Often a stigma or some characteristic used in identifying someone so that they more easily fit into someone's schema of a particular "type" of person. Examples might include a "drunk," a homeless person, someone on "Welfare," or someone of a particular racial or ethnic group.

**Labeling Theory.** A theory used to explain crime by first explaining deviance. The theory suggests that people are labeled based on some action or attitude, which is perceived as deviant. Those labeled as deviant then internalize the attitudes of others and this reinforces the deviance. There are two stages in the labeling process: (1) primary deviance is the initial act that is labeled as deviant by others, and (2) secondary deviance which is when the individual accepts the deviant label.

**Labor-Market Segmentation.** The division of the labor market based on race, ethnicity, or gender.

**Labor Theory of Value.** Karl Marx's theory that the all value (i.e., referring to material goods and their subsequent value) comes from the "have-nots."

**Laissez-Faire Economics.** Laissez-faire in French means "leave alone" and sometimes translated as "hands off." Adam Smith's theory that economic systems develop best when left alone by governments and develop as a result of market forces.

**Language.** Language is comprised of words, which are always symbolic representations of tangible or intangible things.

**Laissez-Faire Leadership Style.** There are generally five types of leadership styles: (1) instrumental, (2) expressive, (3) authoritarian, (4) democratic, and (5) laissez-faire. In French, laissez-faire means to "leave alone" or "hands off." Generally, leaders who effectively use this style work with highly creative and independent subordinates—for instance, the software industry. As much as possible laissez-faire leaders let their subordinates make most of their own decisions. This style of leadership does not work in all situations.

**Latent Function.** Latent functions are unintended functions whereas manifest functions are intended functions. Associated with structural functionalist theory. For instance, the manifest function of the Native American rain dance is to make it rain, while one latent function is that it increases the cohesiveness of the tribe.

**Latent Pattern Maintenance.** The set of structures that serve to replicate patterns in a system with the least possible effort (in the body, the central nervous system; in society, religion and education).

**Law.** Norms that are widely accepted, formally approved by political institutions, and enforced by the criminal justice system.

**Leader.** A person who is seen as possessing the greatest influence on other's behavior and beliefs.

**Learned Helplessness.** When people have little control over what happens to them, and passively learn to accept what is given and therefore lose their independence. Examples include hospital patients, nursing home patients, internees in Nazi extermination camps during WWII.

**Learning Theory.** A theory that suggests humans learn behaviors that are rewarded or reinforced.

**Legitimate.** There are two types of authority: (1) legitimate authority, and illegitimate authority. All authority is given—authority does not exist without consensus and a willingness on the part of individuals to bestow it. Legitimate authority is when people believe that those to whom they are granting authority have a right to it.

**Legitimation.** Stories that provide a moral basis for human behavior (stories that make it okay to do what we do).

**Leisure.** Those activities that are not work-related, occur distinct from those hours spent working, and are enjoyed as freely chosen activities.

**Lesbian.** A woman who is attracted to another woman sexually and emotionally.

**Liberal Feminism.** Theoretical framework that says that the cause of gender inequality is gender socialization and seeks to bring about equality through legal reform.

**Life Chances.** There are a number of factors that determine the likelihood of a person succeeding in our society. Those factors include family socioeconomic status, race, ethnicity, gender, religion, political affiliation, sexual orientation, work ethic, education, work experience, life experience in general, and social network. The likelihood of a person succeeding or failing as a result of the aforementioned factors are called life chances.

**Life Course.** Refers to a person's life stages from birth to death.

**Life-Course Analysis.** An analysis of the life course stages as they influence socialization.

**Life Expectancy.** Also referred to as longevity. The average number of years a people live from birth.

**Lifestyle.** The way a person lives their life. The possessions they own and their routine behaviors.

**Lobbying.** Lobbyists try to influence politicians to support their client's interests.

**Lombroso, Cesare.** Considered the father of modern criminology, Cesare Lombroso (1835 – 1909) (right) was an Italian physician who researched criminals in Italian prisoners in the 1870s. After studying inmates in prison, primarily by performing autopsies on the bodies of convicts, Lombroso concluded there were something he referred to as "born" criminals—in other words, criminals were born with physical characteristics, distinguishable features that separated them from the general population (e.g., low foreheads, prominent jaws, protruding ears, hairiness, emaciated, walked bent over with unusually long arms that dangled at their sides). He referred to "born" criminal as the atavistic criminal.

Lombroso had significant methodological problems with this early research. The largest methodological fault was that he had no control group—in other words, he didn't investigate the physical characteristics of the non-institutionalized general population. Had he done so, he would have found the same features or physical characteristics. However, after publishing his initial research, became world-renowned because they gave the world what they wanted—the ability to look at someone and know if they were a "born" criminal, though as I've stated, this simply wasn't the case because of the methodological flaws in his research.

**Loneliness.** Having a small social network that provides little in the way of stimulation, involvement, and emotional support. While essentials of life may lead to someone being able to survive, loneliness can lead to what is referred to clinically as failure to thrive. See also, social isolation.

**Looking-Glass Self.** Cooley's concept of the looking glass self suggests that people develop their self-image (i.e., the self) from social interactions and feedback from others. Cooley identified three steps involved in the process he conceptualized as the looking glass self in his book *Human Nature and the Social Order (1902)*: (1) the imagination of our appearance to others, (2) the imagination of his judgement of that appearance, and (3) some sort of self-feeling, such as pride or mortification.

**Love.** Love is perhaps one of the most widely used terms, but at the same time, least understood and hardest to define. It's meaning is largely culturally and individually defined. Commonalities in the definition of love include: love should be both partner's selfless dedication to the other, should involve romance, commitment, and be enduring. When a relationship ends, not only does love usually end, but there is a strong belief among former partners that love never actually existed between them. Building on symbolic interaction, and the social construction of reality, this latter belief associates the concept of love to the subjective belief that love endures, and if it does not endure, there was a misinterpretation of symbols by one or both ex-partners that led to the false conclusion that love existed when in fact it never did.

There are many types of love. Romantic love is perhaps the most commonly identified type of love. Yet, it is perhaps the youngest of the different types of love.

**Low-Ball Technique.** A social psychological term for gaining compliance of another by understating the significance of that person's initial compliance.

**Low Culture.** Activities enjoyed by the uneducated and unsophisticated masses that are thought to be of low quality.

**Luddism.** One result of the industrial revolution was the development of machines, driven by water or steam power which often replaced workers. This new technological development that led to the displacement of workers resulted in a form of militancy called Luddism. Luddites would break into factories and destroy machinery in an effort to stop the spread of these new technologies. Today the term is often used to refer to people whom are resistant to new technologies like computers, cellular phones, social media.

**Luhmann, Niklas.** Niklas Luhmann (1927 – 1998) (right) was a German sociologist known for his work on systems theory.

**Lumpenproletariat.** In Marx's view of stratification, he proposed that there were at the time of his writings, three noteworthy classes: (1) the "haves," or the owners of the means of production, (2) a middle class of doctors and merchants, and (3) the "have-nots," or those that worked for the "haves." However, he additionally proposed a fourth class he called the lumpenproletariat. The latter class was below the "have-nots" and Marx believed that not only were they materially below the "have-nots," but were also beneath the concern of even the "have-nots." The modern example of the lumpenproletariat might be the homeless—as a society we don't really "see" them nor do we seem to really care about them. They simply exist.

**Macro Sociology.** Macro sociological theories have wide scale applicability in that they can be used to study many phenomena that are large in their scope like large social structures and institutions. For instance, structural functionalism and the conflict perspective, both of which are examples of macro theories, can be used to study phenomenon like racial, gender or income inequality. Micro sociological theories on the other hand can only be used to study one-on-one social interactions and therefore have very limited applicability—for instance, Homans' social exchange theory.

**Mandatory Arrest Policy.** Refers to intimate partner violence. In cases of domestic abuse, police who respond to a suspected domestic abuse call are obligated by law to have to take one party to jail if there are visible injuries to the other party. In cases where both parties may have visible injuries, both may be go to jail. Prior to a mandatory arrest policy, police could only arrest someone for suspected domestic abuse if they saw the violent act taking place. When it was first proposed in Minnesota, a mandatory arrest policy was resisted by women's groups because they feared a male abuser who had been taken to jail and then released would seek revenge on the abused party. However, the research found just the opposite happened—the likelihood of the violence reoccurring after a mandatory arrest dropped dramatically. Today a mandatory arrest policy is standard in most municipalities.

**Manifest Function.** Manifest functions are intended functions whereas latent functions are unintended functions. Associated with structural functionalist theory. For instance, the manifest function of the Native American rain dance is to make it rain, while one latent function is that it increases the cohesiveness of the tribe.

**Maquiladoras.** Factories located along the Mexican-U.S. border that are in free trade zones and employ mostly young women to work for low wages; used as an example of offshoring.

**Marking (our territory).** The final component of body language is marking our territory. Dogs may mark their territory by peeing on things, but fortunately humans do not. However, we do still mark our territory just in different ways-- positioning our possessions around us to keep people from sitting next to us, always using the same parking space, positioning others at a certain distance from us.

**Marriage.** A legally recognized and approved sexual relationship between two people who are committed to one another.

**Marriage Squeeze.** In the U.S., for every 48 males there are 52 females. A marital squeeze could be said to exist in that females outnumber the supply of males available for marriage.

**Martineau, Harriet.** Harriet Martineau (1802 – 1876) (right) was born in England and became a leading social theorist and critic. She is often referred to as the first female sociologist. Martineau believed that the social conditions of women's lives should be included in the study of sociology and in particular issues of marriage, children, and family. Martineau published a number of books  including *Society in America* (1837), in which she describes the social and political place of women in America. On her visit to America in (1834), she supported Northern abolitionists in their efforts to abolish slavery in the U.S. and often visited with then president James Madison.

**Marx, Karl.** Karl Marx was born May 5, 1818, in Trier, Germany. Spending his life in Germany, France, and England, Marx was a philosopher, social reformist, and revolutionary. Marx is known for his work on the political economy in which he espoused the belief that capitalism as an ideology caused divisions between people, Marx believed that social change resulted only from economic  influences and that society, uninfluenced by capitalism, was naturally cohesive. In sociology, he is known for what is called the conflict perspective which is a macro theory.

**Marxian Approach.** One of the major theoretical perspectives in sociology and emphasizes the importance of unequal power and conflict in society. Based on the writings of Karl Marx, Marxist theory centers around the idea that capitalism breeds conflict—a class struggle for scarce resources between the workers (i.e., the have-nots) and the owners (i.e., the owners of the means of production). Proposing that society was a system based on inequality and conflict, Marx wrote: "The history of all hitherto existing society is the history of class struggles."

**Masculinity.** Sex refers to the biological distinctions between males and females. Gender refers to the roles and behaviors of males and females that are culturally defined. Masculinity refers to specific behaviors and roles culturally assigned to men, but in reality, demonstrated by both males and females to varying degrees. For instance, in our culture men are not expected to cry, but some men do—some while at the funeral of a loved one and others while watching a sad movie.

**Mass Culture.** The media and other consumer and cultural products that are designed for consumption by the masses and which can be a source of manipulation and exploitation by the elite.

**Mass Hysteria.** Collective fears or anxiety from perceived threats resulting from rumors, imagination, or psychosis. While explanations are still contentious, the Salem Witch Trials (1692 – 1693), which resulted in the deaths of 25 people who were found guilty of witchcraft, is thought to have resulted from mass hysteria. Four young girls, Abigail Williams, Betty Parris, Ann Putnam, and Elizabeth Hubbard, began to have what was described as "fits." When questioned, the girls indicated they were afflicted by Satan as a result of their interactions with a slave girl named Tituba. Accusations of witchcraft began to spread throughout Salem and the ensuing trials, using "spectral" evidence, resulted in a number of residents being found guilty of being in league with the Devil.

**Mass Media.** Forms of communication that include magazines, books, television, television commercials, radio, the Internet, and movies.

**Mass Society.** Typical of industrialized societies, mass societies are characterized by impersonality, isolation, and one in which individual achievement is highly valued.

**Master Status.** The status that society regards as the most important of the many statuses a person holds. For instance, success (i.e., wealth), gender, race or ethnicity, occupation.

**Matching Hypothesis.** The belief that people are attracted to others who are judged similar to them and at the same level of desirability.

**Material Culture.** Those components of culture which are tangible and easily seen.

**Material Deprivation.** The inability to purchase material goods due to a lack of money.

**Matriarchy.** Female dominance in a society.

**Matrilocal.** A cultural expectation that married couples live with the wife's family.

**McDonaldization.** The belief, according to sociologist George Ritzer, that the processes used by the fast-food industry have come to dominate the way that society functions. He identifies five functions of the fast-food industry that have been applied to modern life: (1) efficiency, (2) calculability, (3) predictability, (4) control of workers (i.e., people) with the use of technology, and the "irrationality of rationality." Ritzer believes that these functions result in a bureaucratic structure that is easy to replicate in a number of different types of organizations. Generally, this process benefits organizations and higher-level management, but at the expense of lower level workers.

**McVeigh, Timothy.** Timothy James McVeigh (1968 – 2001) (right) was an American terrorist convicted and executed for the bombing of the Oklahoma City Federal Building in 1994. The attack killed 168 people and injured over 600. It was the deadliest act of terrorism within the U.S. before the 9/11 attacks. McVeigh defended his action as revenge for the federal government's action during the siege of the Branch Davidian compound outside of Waco, Texas.

**Me.** George Herbert Mead (1863 - 1931) in his theory of the development of the self, defines the "me" is that part of the self that understands the norms, beliefs, and attitudes of the society in which they live. The "me" is a person's acceptance and perception of the generalized other. See also, generalized other.

**Mead, G.H.** George Herbert Mead (1863 – 1931) was a sociologist who is credited for being the creator of symbolic interactionism. Mead proposed that our "self" (i.e., self-awareness) was the result of social interaction. Mead believed that as children we pass through three stages as we develop our sense of self. Those three stages are:

- **Preparatory Stage:** By the age of two years, children are able to mimic the behaviors of others in their social world even though they lack understanding what those behaviors mean.
- **Play Stage**: Between the ages of two and six years, children began to role-play which then allows them to take on the roles of important people in their social world.
- **Game Stage**: By the age of seven years and older, children have learned what their role is in their social world while they continue to be able to take on the roles of others as if in a game.

**Mean.** When a total sum is calculated and then divided by the number of cases, we have a mean. The mean is what most Americans think of as "average." See also, Mode and Median.

> Given the following score distribution: 10, 11, 11, 12, 14, 15, and 16.
>
> Mean = 12.7
> Median = 12.0
> Mode = 11
> Range = 6

**Means of Consumption.** According to Marx, the means of consumption are the consumer goods manufactured by the "have-nots" and which financially benefit the "haves" via the labor of the "have-nots." However, George Ritzer, takes Marx's attitude further by suggesting that the means of consumption also refers to those things that make consumption possible—for instance, mass production and efficient distribution to the consumer.

**Means of Production.** Those things owned by the "haves" that are needed for the production of material goods (e.g., raw materials, tools, machinery, and factories).

**Mechanical Solidarity.** Émile Durkheim believed that social cohesion was based on social connections from shared experiences like knowledge, education, work skills, and religion. He called this social cohesion mechanical solidarity. On the other hand, organic solidarity is defined as social cohesion that is based on dependence and interdependence that exists in modern industrialized societies.

**Median.** The median is the midpoint of a score distribution; half of all scores fall on one side of the median and half fall on the other side. See also, mean.

**Medicaid.** A federally funded program designed to provide aid to people with lower income.

**Medicalization of Deviant Behavior.** Defining behavior as the result of a medical condition allowing for medical intervention and treatment; a means of social control (as when homosexuality was defined as an illness).

**Medicare.** A federally funded health insurance program for senior citizens who receive Social Security benefits.

**Melting Pot.** A term that usually refers to a society that has assimilated. Often misused when applied to pluralistic societies. See also, assimilation.

**Menstrual Taboos.** Subordinate women by segregating them from the rest of society when they have their cycle. Menstruation is considered "unclean."

**Mere Exposure Effect.** The belief that mere exposure to objects and others will lead to greater positive feelings towards those objects or other individuals. Sometimes associated with theories that address how to reduce levels of prejudice towards people judged in a person's outgroup.

**Meritocracy.** A system where people are awarded status based on their individual efforts. See also, achieved status.

**Meta-Analysis.** The belief that by attempting to use different studies and different methodologies to discover facts about what is being studied leads to a greater and more accurate understanding that which is being studied. See also, research triangulation.

**Methodology.** Refers to research methodology. The type of research method that is used to investigate phenomenon. A research method has a set of rules and procedures for collecting facts. Examples include survey research, participant observation, experimental research, and field research.

**Metropolitan Statistical Area (MSA).** A geographical area containing either one city with 50,000 or more residents or an urban area of at least 50,000 inhabitants and a total population of at least 100,000 (except in New England where the required total is 75,000).

**Microaggressions.** Subtle words, behavior and ideas that are expressed in daily interactions, when a person from a majority or dominant group evokes a stereotype or passes judgement on minority or marginalized groups. Microaggressions may be informed by overt prejudice or by unconscious bias.

**Micro Sociology.** Micro sociological theories can only be used to study one-on-one social interactions and therefore have very limited applicability—for instance, Homans' social exchange theory. On the other hand, macro sociological theories have wide scale applicability in that they can be used to study many phenomena that are large in their scope like large social structures and institutions. For instance, structural functionalism and the conflict perspective, both of which are examples of macro theories, can be used to study phenomenon like racial, gender or income inequality.

**Middle Class.** The middle strata in a class system. Usually made up of white-collar workers.

**Middle-Range Theories.** Theories that attempt to seek the middle-ground between macro theories, which have broad applicability, and micro theories, which have very limited applicability.

**Milgram, Stanley.** Stanley Milgram (1933 - 1984) was an American social psychologist. Between 1933 and 1945, Nazis murdered 11 million Jews and people from other "undesirable" groups. Fascinated by one the most notorious Nazis responsible for the Holocaust, Milgram wanted to know if people in general would be more likely to commit horrendous acts because they would obey authority. To test his theory, Milgram conducted his research on obedience in the early 1960 at Yale university. Milgram found that approximately 2/3s of his male research subjects were willing to administer 450 volt shocks to a victim, despite the fact that the victim wanted to stop participating after receiving a 150-volt shock, simply because they were told to do so by a perceived authority figure (i.e., a male researcher dressed in a white lab coat). Unbeknownst to those administering the shocks, the victim wasn't really being shocked—the victim simply acted the part, using protests and screams of pain, so no one was really hurt.

Milgram's research has been repeated at different locations throughout the U.S. and around the world, and the results have always been found to be the same. However, Milgram was criticized for his work because some of his subjects who administered the pretend shocks complained later of having psychological issues as a consequence of having participated in the research. While Milgram felt the criticism was overblown, his research led to the creation of Institutional Review Boards designed to protect the rights of research participants.

**Mills, C. Wright.** C. Wright Mills (1916 – 1962) was an American sociologist known for his Sociological Imagination and the Power Elite. Mills was a conflict theorist and approached class divisions and inequality in the U.S. from that point of view. In the Power Elite (1956), Mills wrote how power in the U.S. was centralized in the hands of a small group of powerful and rich people, who came from one or several influential groups (i.e., politicians, military, and upper classes), tended to be male, white, Protestant, share the same general social upbringing, and tended to socialize with each other. Because of these similarities and interactions, they tended to share the same general agenda for the U.S., and that shared view or agenda was what came them power collectively. While Americans believe that they 'run' America by the act of voting in a democracy, Mills adamantly disagreed stating that power was in fact in the hands of the aforementioned power elite.

**Minority Group.** Heterogeneous societies (e.g., U.S., U.K., Canada, and most European countries) will have a dominant group and other groups; homogenous societies only have a dominant group (e.g., Japan). Minority groups are those groups that have some identifiable feature (e.g., race, ethnicity, religion) that makes them different from the dominant group in some way. Minority groups tend to share the same cultural heritage and think of themselves as sharing special bonds. Further, minority groups think of themselves as being singled out for discrimination on the basis of the aforementioned features. Examples of minority groups include African-Americans, Hispanic Americans, Native Americans, and Asian Americans.

**Minority Influence.** A process where dissenters or deviants from the group norm may lead to a change of belief or behavior within a group. For instance, in the classic American movie "Twelve Angry Men," the actor Henry Fonda's character dissents with other members of the jury initially but with his use of logic and reason reverses the jury's opinion.

**Mobilization.** Refers to Neil Smelser's name for the process by which people come together to engage in some kind of collective action.

**Mode.** Simply put, the most common score in a distribution. See also, Mean and Median.

**Modernity.** An historical era in which urbanization and industrialization play key roles.

**Modernization.** The social and economic process by which pre-industrial societies modernize to an industrialized society.

**Modern Societies.** There are four types of modern societies: (1) first world, (2) second world, (3) third world, and (4) societies that are in the process of industrializing. Characteristics for the four modern societies are:

- First world. Eighteenth century to the present. Based on industrialization and the majority of the population lives in cities where the industry is located. Agricultural production is mechanized. First world societies are generally highly stratified. First world countries include Western nations, Japan, Australia, and New Zealand.

- Second world. Early to late twentieth century. Generally, these are former countries of the Soviet Union.

- Third world. Eighteenth century to the present. These countries are agricultural based and tend to export more than they import.

- Newly industrializing countries. Countries evolving from third world, and sometimes second world countries. As these countries industrialize, they move away from their agricultural base.

**Monarchy.** A country ruled by a king or queen and power is passed down within the monarchy from one generation to the next.

**Monogamy.** Two people in a romantic and sexual relationship who are exclusively committed to each other.

**Monopoly.** The exclusive control and dominance of a sector by an organization.

**Monotheism.** A belief in one god. Of the world's largest religions, three are Abrahamic religions: Judaism, Christianity, and Islam.

**Moral Reasoning.** Resulting largely from the process of socialization, the beliefs people have about what they consider right or wrong. See also, socialization.

**Mores.** Social norms that when violated carry sanctions which may be formal (i.e., legal proceedings in civil or criminal court) or informal.

**Mortality Rate.** The number of deaths per thousand in a population.

**Mosuo People.** In the Chinese province of Yunnan, in Southern China, there is a mountain lake called Lugu Lake and the people who live around the lake are called the Mosuo people. The Mosuo people practice what is the only matriarchal society in existence in the world—though some suggest it is not fully matriarchal because men still dominate in positions of power. Female Mosuo are usually the head of the house, make business decisions, and the bloodline is passed down through them. The Mosuo people practice what is called a "walking marriage." Women in the Mosuo culture signal to a man they are interested in them. When the man accepts a woman's invitation to go home with her, he will have sex with her, and if she becomes pregnant, the man will live with the woman until she gives birth. After giving birth, the male will leave the home and the father's role will go to her brother.

**Multicultural Society.** Societies that are made up of multiple ethnic groups.

**Multinational Corporation.** A corporation that has business operations in multiple countries.

**Nation.** A political and geographical area in which people share a common language and cultural history, but the final resting place of power is beyond the nation. For instance, the Cherokee Nation is a nation because, while tribal members share a common language and cultural history, the final resting place of power is Washington, D.C.

**Nation-State.** A political and geographical area in which people share a common language and cultural history and the final resting place of power is within the nation. For example, Japan.

**Nationalism.** A belief in the superiority of a nation and that attempts to solidify individual members of that nation into a cohesive set of beliefs.

**Naturalistic Observation.** A research method in which investigators study behavior within the setting in which it occurs as opposed to a laboratory setting.

**Natural Selection.** The basic argument of evolution. The belief that organisms that have biological features which provide a better fit with their natural environment are more likely to reproduce and thrive in that particular environment whereas organisms that have features that are not well-suited for adaptation with that environment are more likely to die out.

**Nature Versus Nurture.** Nature refers to those things about people that is entirely the result of biology. Examples would include height, hair color, eye color, and predispositions to specific illnesses. Nurture refers to the environment—in other words, what is learned or experienced through socialization and interaction with others. With the exception of those aforementioned specific biological factors, our behaviors fall along a continuum where nature is at one extreme and nurture at the other extreme. Researchers often use twin studies (i.e., identical twins separated at birth) to answer questions about whether a behavior is the result of nature or nurture. Some examples of behaviors that are a combination of both nature and nurture are listed below.

- **IQ.** An intelligence quotient (IQ) is a score thought to assess human intelligence. Research has found that the environment, especially the lack of social interaction and stimulation, can significantly retard the genetic potential of IQ.

- **Schizophrenia.** Schizophrenia is a mental disorder that affects how a person thinks, feels and acts. Schizophrenics may have difficulty distinguishing between what is real and what is imaginary, may be unresponsive or withdrawn, and may have difficulty expressing normal emotions in social situations. It is thought that child sexual abuse prior to the age of four could trigger schizophrenia in adulthood when there is no biological predisposition for the illness.
- **Depression.** While there are different types of depression, the most common symptom for all types of depression is sadness that lasts for several weeks or longer. While there are biological factors that can contribute to depression, like low levels of serotonin and dopamine, there are also environmental factors that can lead to depression—for instance, losing a loved one, unemployment, and financial problems.
- **Alcoholism.** Alcoholism is characterized by loss of control over the use of alcohol and withdrawal symptoms if someone stops drinking for some period of time. While there are biological factors that put certain people at greater risk for alcoholism, environmental factors can play a part as well. For instance, the choices people make.
- **Aggression/violence.** While aggression is linked to testosterone, and so there is a biological factor involved in aggression, the environment can also affect aggression and violence levels—for example, stress, frustration, and having learned aggression as a problem-solving strategy.

**Need for Cognition.** A mental characteristic of humans to want to think. Need for cognitive stimulation.

**Needs.** Essentially, those things that people need to survive. Needs drive consumption.

**Negative Sanction.** A formal or informal punishment applied to persons who deviate from social norms.

**Negative State Relief Model.** A psychological concept that suggests that when people are experiencing negative emotions about themselves, may have experience positive self-emotions when helping others.

**Negativity Bias.** The tendency of people to attach more importance to negative features of others rather than to positive traits. There are many causes of negativity bias including prejudice, in-group favoritism, and confirmation bias.

**Negotiation.** A form of social interaction in which two or more parties in conflict or competition arrive at a mutually satisfactory agreement.

**Neo-Colonialism.** The exploitation of third-world countries by the most powerful industrialized countries for their resources.

**Neolocality.** A system in which married couples live in their own home as opposed to living in his or her parent's home.

**Neo-Tribes.** Often associated with fads and trends forming loose associations among followers, which are often short in duration.

**Network (social).** A social network is made up of both strong and weak ties. Strong ties would be those people who have direct and supportive links to all persons in the particular social network, while weak ties refer to members of a social network who have ties with people outside the network, but those ties assist others in the network in some way—for instance, with information. A social network is a social structure in which ongoing social interactions between members occur.

**Networking.** An activity in which people who are like-minded or have common interests interact with the outcome being potentially physically or economically beneficial to the actors.

**New Money.** Generally used to refer to a class of people who have improved their status from that of their parent's and are considered wealthy or upper-class. See also, achieved status.

**Nobility.** The highest stratum in an estate system of stratification (e.g., lords and viscounts) usually with a monarch ruling the country. Power and title are passed down from one generation to the next.

**Nomadic.** Hunting and gathering and pastoral societies are nomadic in that they periodically move from one place to another as they use up available resources and therefore must move to another location where more resources are available.

**Nonmaterial Culture.** Those components of culture that are not tangible and not easily seen such as norms and values.

**Nonverbal Behavior.** A method of using nonverbal symbols to communicate someone's intentions and/or feelings to others.

**Nonverbal Communication.** Symbols that are communicated (and interpreted) without words. Nonverbal symbols include two categories: (1) body language, and (2) physical characteristics. Body language would include such components as body movement, eye contact, civil inattention, interpersonal space, and marking territory. Physical characteristics would include the biological image (e.g., race, gender, height, weight, hair color, eye color), and the made image (e.g., how one dresses, the car they drive, the home they live in).

**Norm.** The do's and don'ts of a culture. Normative expectations that apply to behavior, appearance, and verbal statements.

**Norm of Social Justice.** A tendency to help those we feel deserve to be helped.

**Norm of Social Responsibility.** A norm acting on the human conscious to help others who are in need.

**Normal Science.** All sciences follow the scientific method to collect facts about some phenomenon. The last step in the scientific method is to disseminate or publish the research results. By publishing research findings, this is how any science builds their body of knowledge because the published research then may become a foundation for future research investigating similar research themes.

**Normative Influence.** Actions performed to achieve some goal or avoid punishment. Examples include conformity and obedience.

**Normative Organization.** Formal organization that individuals join in order to promote an important social cause. Most voluntary organizations are considered normative.

**Nuclear Family.** The nuclear family is the idealized notion of family life in America. A nuclear family consists of a married couple and their children. The other type of family unity, and is the more typical of the two, is the extended family. The extended family consists of the adult couple, their children, elderly parents of the adult couple, possibly, siblings of the adult couple, aunts, uncles, cousins, and more all living under the same roof.

**Nye, Ivan.** Ivan Nye (1918 – 2014) was an American sociologist associated with social control theory. Nye developed 12 theoretical propositions that helped explain social exchange theory.

- Individuals choose those alternatives that have the highest potential for profit.
- Cost being equal, they choose alternatives which have the highest potential for profit.
- Rewards being equal, they choose alternatives which have the least

- potential for costs.
- Immediate outcomes being equal, they choose those alternatives that will likely have the best long-term outcomes.
- Long-term outcomes being perceived as equal, they choose alternatives with the highest potential for the best short-term profits.
- Costs and other rewards being equal, individuals choose the alternatives that are likely to provide the most potential for the most social approval.
- Costs and other rewards being equal, individuals choose statuses and relationships that have the highest potential for autonomy.
- Other rewards and costs equal, individuals choose alternatives that have the least ambiguity in terms of expected future events and outcomes.
- Other costs and rewards equal, they choose alternatives that have the most potential to provide the most security for them.
- Other rewards and costs equal, they choose to associate with, marry, and form other relationships with those whose values and opinions generally are in agreement and reject or avoid those with whom they disagree.
- Other rewards and costs equal, they are more likely to associate with, marry, and form other relationships with their equals.
- In industrial societies, other costs and rewards equal, individuals choose alternatives that promise the greatest financial gains.

**Obedience.** Obedience is conformity or compliance with a perceived higher and legitimate authority. Research has found that good and honest people may not even consider behavior that is 'unthinkable' as that good and honest person, but acting under the orders of someone perceived to have legitimate authority over them carry out brutal and unthinkable acts without hesitation. See also, Stanley Milgram.

**Objectivity.** Procedures or methods researchers follow to minimize bias in observation or misinterpretation due to personal or social values. Research reports, usually in the methods section, describe the procedures used by those researchers to arrive at their research facts. These sections are usually so detailed that other researchers can duplicate their study, and hopefully verify their findings. In the discussion section of a standard research report, researchers are expected to be self-critical and point out the limitations and strengths of their research in an objective manner. Also, it is customary for researchers to suggest future research agendas that answer questions the former researchers forgot to do and/or to further the study of the particular phenomenon under investigation. By publishing their work, researchers allow other researchers working in the field to closely examine and question the methods used to discover those research facts, and the evidence for the researcher's conclusions.

**Observational Research.** Sometimes referred to as field research, it is a type of correlational research in which the researcher observes some kind of ongoing behavior that is being studied.

**Observer Bias.** A key principle of scientific research is that it is supposed to be objective and without bias. When dealing with human researchers, this is more an ideal than a reality. Observer bias is when researchers bring in their own preconceived notions about the research or the research outcome and thus introduce bias, which reduces the strength of the research findings.

**Occupational Segregation.** The segregation of workers in the paid labor force by gender, race, and ethnicity. However, research clearly demonstrates that the chief reason people face discrimination and unequal treatment in the workforce is based on gender.

**Occupational Socialization.** Socialization that occurs in the workplace.

**Oligarchy.** Within a group, organization, or society it is the rule by few rather by the many. In 2016, Bernie Sanders, a presidential candidate wrote, "This is what oligarchy looks like: Today, the top one-tenth of 1 percent owns almost as much wealth as the bottom 90 percent. The top one-hundreth of 1 percent makes more than 40 percent of all campaign contributions. The billionaire class owns the political system and reaps the benefits from it."

**One-drop Rule.** Originated in the American South and was eventually adopted by the entire nation. It stated that if a person had even one drop of African blood in their ancestry, they were African American.

**Operant Conditioning.** Essentially, operant conditioning refers to the learning process as being the result of the consequences of a given behavior as modifying that behavior. Behavior is generally reinforced if followed by a reward and most likely extinguished if followed by a punishment.

**Operationalization.** In research, operationalization is the process of making a variable testable. To do so, researchers need to be highly specific in how they choose to measure that variable. Operationalizing a variable reduces the potential for bias introduced when (1) subjects might be confused by research questions, and (2) researchers are unclear what respondents have reported. For instance, if we wanted to know about someone's income we might ask, "What is your individual, gross, annual income in US dollars? If income is our variable, we have fully operationalized it with the aforementioned measurement.

Another example might be if we were interested in studying the relationship between income and physical health, we would need to operationalize both of these variables. As an example, let's operationalize the variable income.

    First attempt: How much money do you make?

    Second attempt: What is your annual income?

    Third attempt: What is your annual individual income?

Fourth attempt: What is your annual individual net income?

**Opportunity Costs.** Rational choice theory suggests that people must choose between two or more options when trying to achieve some end or goal. When one option is selected, the next most desirable option, though not selected, becomes a foregone opportunity.

**Oppositional Culture.** Culture or way of life where norms, values, and beliefs are in opposition to mainstream culture; in many oppositional cultures, acts of deviance are rewarded.

**Ordinal Variables.** Ordinal and categorical variables are similar in some respects; however, they differ in the way the two order the variables. For instance, if economic status was your variable, you might have three statuses: low, medium, and high.

**Organic Solidarity.** In societies with a complex division of labor, collective consciousness creates on mutual interdependence.

**Organismic Analogy.** Thinking about society as if it worked just like an organism.

**Organization.** A social group, small or large, that has explicit values and sought-after goals—including those for its continued existence.

**Organizational Ritualism.** In bureaucracies, workers tend to lose sight of the purpose for the rules, policies, and practices because they have little autonomy, are not encouraged to think beyond those rules and regulations, and the overriding order to employees is simply to follow the clearly established policies established by the bureaucracy. In other words, bureaucrats go through the motions without understanding why they go through those motions.

**Outgroup.** In groups are those groups to which we think are alike in some way; outgroups, on the other hand, are made up of people we feel are significantly different than us in some way—and while researchers understand these differences are usually superficial, generally people do not fail to see them as superficial, but rather as crucial. For instance, a white person might feel that other white persons share some important characteristic with them that separates them from African-Americans if they are perceived as an outgroup. In-groups versus outgroups are highly associated with prejudice, discrimination, and even conflict.

**Outgroup Homogeneity Effect.** The belief that people in another's outgroup tend to be more alike than people in their own in-group.

**Outsourcing.** The relocation of jobs from one country to another in order to reduce overall costs.

**Paradigm.** In sociology, a paradigm is similar to a theory in that it offers explanations that help to understand and predict social behavior.

**Parallel Marriage.** An egalitarian marriage in which both husbands and wives share the division of household tasks. This is more likely when husbands and wives have approximately the same educational level, similar familial backgrounds, feel mutually financially dependent on the other, respect each other and their contributions to the household, and are progressive rather than traditional in mindset.

**Parsons, T.** (1902 – 1979). Talcott Parsons was an American sociologist known for his *Structure of Social Action* (1937) in which he first set out his general theory of action. In 1951, he refined his general theory of action in two seminal works: *Social System* and *Towards a General Theory of Action*. Parson thought of his general theory of action as being applicable to all social behavior throughout  history. Though Parsons thought referring to his theoretical ideas as structural functionalism was too simplistic, he was however responsible for bringing Max Weber's work to the U.S. In looking at society as a system, and with survival and equilibrium as crucial for the system, Parsons believed there were four important components necessary to fulfil those goals: (1) social systems must adapt to changes in their environment or die; (2) systems must have clearly stated goals; (3) elements of the system must work together and work within the overarching greater system; and (4) the system must maintain norms and values which justify the actions within the system.

**Participant Observation.** A research method in which the researcher observes while taking part in the activities of the social group being studied to some level of involvement—that involvement ranges from pure observation and therefore no involvement to the other end of the spectrum where there is pure observation and involvement. There are four roles of participant observation:

- Complete participant. In complete participation, the researcher completely engages with the group being studied and their true identity is hidden from the group.

- Participant as observer. In participant as observer, the researcher engages with the group, but makes no pretense as their true identity as researchers.

- Observer as participant. In this type of participant observation, the researcher observes, but does not participate.

- Complete observer. In this situation, the researcher is completely detached from the group being studied and simply records observations for future analysis. For instance, a researcher might decide to sit in a corner of a bar and record their observations of how people act when in a bar while drinking and socializing with others.

**Participatory Democracy.** Participatory democracy (direct democracy) occurs when everyone is involved in all decision making. The U.S. practices representative democracy and not participatory democracy. Many people advocate the adoption of participatory democracy because computer and communication technologies make direct democracy (i.e., every citizen votes on every issue) possible—though practicality may be another matter. The only recorded society that practiced participatory democracy was ancient Greece—though only wealthy landowners were allowed to participate in this form of democracy.

**Passionate Love.** The state of intense longing for the object of a person's love and affection. Researchers have noted that the characteristics of passionate love, also known as being in-love, mirror the characteristics of being high on drugs and mental illness.

**Pastoral Societies.** Mankind went from hunting and gathering to pastoral and then agrarian societies. In agrarian societies man stayed in one place, rather than being nomadic. Pastoral societies were only slightly less nomadic that agrarian societies in that they tended not to move great distances to find areas more suitable for the grazing of their livestock. Marx believed that both agrarian and pastoral societies were essentially without stratification as all tribal or clan members pretty well had the same possessions as they were a liability when moving from one area to the next.

**Patriarchy.** Male dominance in a society. See also, matriarchy.

**Patriarchal Family.** A family in which the husband and father is the formal head of the household.

**Patrilocal.** A culture in which married couples live with the husband's parents.

**Perception Control Theory.** In order for collection action to occur within a society, people must be able to correctly interpret and monitor each other's behavior.

**Peer Group.** Essentially, friends of about the same age and social status who are a reference group and exert influence over members.

**Perception.** According to George Herbert Mead, perception is when an actor searches for ways to satisfy the impulse (second state of an act) and responds accordingly to find ways to deal with it.

**Peripheral Nations.** Low income nations that are dependent on wealthier nations for foreign aid and investment.

**Peripheral Route to Persuasion.** There are two routes of persuasion: the central route, which uses facts and reason, and the peripheral route, which uses emotional appeals.

**Personality.** The organization of behavioral characteristics of a person.

**Personal Space.** The distance that we like to keep others from us based on cultural norms and the nature of the relationship. In the US, research has found that we like to keep strangers at approximately six feet from us, friends around four feet from us, and intimate others at two feet or closer. When violated, we may feel uncomfortable and try to increase the distance to one with which we feel comfortable.

**Persuasion.** Persuasion is the art or ability to get others to perform a behavior or develop an attitude that the persuader wants them to accept or practice. There are two routes used to persuade others: the central route, which utilizes reason and facts, and the peripheral route, which utilizes the use of symbols to evoke emotions.

**Pessimistic Explanatory Style.** When a person sees the loci of their failures as internally caused (i.e., their internal weaknesses or faults), and their successes as externally caused (e.g., luck, the situation).

**Peter Principle.** Developed by Peter and Hull (1969), within organizations, the Peter Principle suggests that people will be promoted to the level of their incompetency. In other words, someone might be given a promotion for doing a specific task well, but by promoting them, they may be raised to a level in which they are inefficient at performing assigned tasks well.

**Physical Attractiveness Stereotype.** A belief furthered by the mass media that more attractive people who possess socially desirable characteristics and features are happier and lead better lives than do people not perceived to be physically attractive.

**Physical Characteristics.** The second component of channels of communication are physical characteristics. Again, these are symbols that are interpreted. The first is our biological image. Our biological image represents those characteristics about us over which we have no control- we are born with those characteristics. Height, eye color, skin color, facial features, gender, and weight to some degree. These are things that we have no control over, but they are interpreted by others. The research is very clear in that tall people are generally perceived to be more competent than short people. Likewise, the research also suggests that attractive people are more favored in the workplace than lesser attractive people. Overweight people, according to the research, are often victims of discrimination. Overweight men, to a certain point are actually favored. Research also suggests that married males are more likely to be promoted and are paid more than single males. The reason for all of these research findings is that these characteristics are interpreted and people treat us according to those interpretations. The number one characteristic that is associated with discrimination in the workplace may surprise you: it's gender. The ratio of males to females in the United States is 48 to 52. As I've mentioned before, all things being equal, we should expect to see that ratio than anything we study. If we have had 44 presidents, and all things were equal, approximately 23 or 24 of those should have been female, but as we all know we have not had one female president to date.

Made images are those things that we have control over. We can change your hair color, we can control the type of clothes that we wear, we can choose the type of car that we want to be seen driving, or the house to live in. Again, those are all symbolic and therefore all interpreted.

**Piaget, J.** Jean Piaget (1896 – 1980) was a Swiss clinical psychologist known for his seminal work in child development, and in particular, his work on the theory of cognitive development. In 1920, after observing children attempting to reason and understand their social world, he found that the ability to reason and understanding differed depending on their age. Piaget proposed that children  progress through a series of cognitive stages of development—akin to how children develop physically. Piaget believed it varies between children to some degree, but at some point, all (normal) children will pass through these stages and in the order Piaget identified them.

Piaget believed that cognitive development resulted from two distinct processes:
    1. adaptation

2. equilibrium

As situational demands on the child change, children will attempt to adapt to these changes by one of two ways:

A. they either assimilate, which involves replacing old concepts with new and more situationally relevant concepts, or accommodation, which involves the
B. expansion and greater understanding of certain already acquired concepts.

Stage: **Sensorimotor** (age 0 – 2). The child learns by doing, looking, touching, and sucking. Begins to understand cause-and-effect relationships.

Stage: **Preoperational** (age 2 – 7). Use of symbols and language. Egocentrism is present.

Stage: **Concrete Operations** (7 – 11). Concrete thinking still present. More mature understanding of cause and effect.

Stage: **Formal Operations** (12+). Ability to use abstract thinking skills, logic, and reasoning.

Because all people and institutions seek equilibrium, Piaget believed that children tried to achieve a balance by adapting to changing situational demands, and as the child ages and moves further along this development path, the child is able to understand and adapt to even more complex changes in their present situation.

**Play.** Activity among children occurring spontaneously, but which rules are imposed and is generally make-believe.

**Play Stage.** Between the ages of two and six years, children began to role-play which then allows them to take on the roles of important people in their social world. See also, Mead, G.H.

**Pluralism.** Also referred to as multiculturalism. A society is pluralistic when all groups, the dominant group and minority groups, value each other's distinctiveness. In other words, people within a given society value the ideal of diversity. The formula often used to express pluralism is: A+B+C=A+B+C – where A represents the dominant group and B and C represent minority groups.

**Polyani, Karl.** Karl Polyani (1886 – 1964) was a Hungarian-American known for his work as a historical sociologist. Polyani proposed the term "substantivism" in his book *The Great Transformation* (1944) to refer to his belief that 'economics' has two meanings. The first refers to economics as the rational choice between alternatives. The second suggests that man attempts to adapt to his changing environmental and material conditions, but not necessarily using rational choice. He proposes that economics should be seen in a broader sense, what he calls provisioning. In Polyani's theory he suggests that economics is a way that society simply meets the demands of material needs.

**Policy Research.** The use of scientific results, primarily results of social scientific research to affect public policy change.

**Political Order.** The recognized authoritative system that acquires and uses legitimate power. It is the social institution that disseminates power, creates a society's agenda, though the political order attempts to get its citizens to believe the agenda is theirs and not of the political order, and makes decisions in regard how to use that power. The political order creates policies and laws and additionally makes decisions affecting the citizenry.

**Political Party.** A political party represents a group of people who identify with particular ideologies and agendas that attempts to use political power to influence political and social policy decisions.

**Polity.** Another word for government.

**Polyandry.** A system where a woman can have more than one husband.

**Polygyny.** A system where a man can have more than one wife.

**Polygamy.** A system where someone can have multiple spouses. See also, polyandry and polygyny.

**Polytheism.** A belief in many gods. One example would be Hinduism.

**Popular Culture.** Aspects of cultural components that are used and enjoyed by the masses. Examples would include television shows, magazines, sports, electronic games and others.

**Population (of study).** In demography, all the people living in a given geographic area. In research, the total number of cases with a particular characteristic.

**Population Exclusion.** The efforts of the dominant societal group to prevent minority groups from joining or assimilating into it.

**Population Transfer.** A type of expulsion, the dominant group attempts to relocate or remove (possibly through genocide) members of a minority group.

**Positive Sanctions.** While sanctions are usually used to refer to punishments, positive sanctions refer to rewards for some socially desirable behavior.

**Positivist.** An approach to explaining human action that does not take into account the individual's interpretation of the situation.

**Post Modernity.** An historical period in which mass media and advertising play key roles.

**Post-Test.** A test given after respondents are given an initial test and then exposed to a research treatment. The post-test, when compared to pretest results, will determine if there has been a change in behavior or attitude of the respondents because of the exposure to the research treatment.

**Postindustrial Society.** Daniel Bell (1919 – 2011) was an American sociologist who believed that postindustrial societies are organized around information and knowledge and not merely industrial production. In these postindustrial societies, utilizing an information-based economy, greater social inequality has increased. This then has led to further social stratification (inequality). The greatest percentage of workers in postindustrial societies work in service industries, which is largely the result of knowledge and information, but few people continue to work in industry.

**Post-Traumatic Shock Disorder (P.T.S.D.).** Once called shell shock or battle fatigue, PTSD is a serious condition that can develop after a person has experienced or witnessed a traumatic or terrifying event. While normally this requires that the PTSD victim experienced some physical harm (e.g., war or a violent act related to crime) some research suggests that emotional harm may also lead to PTSD. In addition to consequences of war and crime victimization, divorce is now identified as a possible source of PTSD. It can lead to unwarranted helplessness, horror, or intense fear about sexual or physical assault, the unexpected death of a loved one, an accident, war, or natural disaster. PTSD victims may have serious reactions like shock, anger, nervousness, fear, and even guilt. Generally, PTSD is difficult to treat and its consequences could be life long and make living a normal life virtually impossible.

**Poverty.** There are two types of poverty measures: relative and absolute. A relative measure of poverty would examine how much any one person or household had in comparison to the average individuals or households had in that society. However, relative poverty might identify someone as poor with an income of $50,000 per year if the mean income for the community or society is $75,000 per year. But can an individual live on $50,000 a year? Of course, and in relative comfort. So that doesn't seem to be the best measure of poverty. What is needed is something that measures how much individuals and families need to survive and that is what an absolute measure of poverty does—it takes into account the costs of those things necessary for survival like food, shelter, medical costs, transportation costs, clothing, and other items. The condition of having too little income to buy the necessities-- food, shelter, clothing, and/or healthcare is called absolute poverty.

**Power.** The ability of one person to get another person to do their will. The ability to get what one person wants within a group despite resistance.

**Power Elite.** C. Wright Mills (1916 – 1962) was an American sociologist who was known for his work titled *Power Elite (1956)*. Mills was a conflict theorist and approached class divisions and inequality in the U.S. from that point of view. He wrote how power in the U.S. was centralized in the hands of a small group of powerful and rich people, who came from one or several influential groups (i.e., politicians, military, and upper classes), tended to be male, white, Protestant, share the same general social upbringing, and tended to socialize with each other. Because of these similarities and interactions, they tended to share the same general agenda for the U.S., and that shared view or agenda was what came them power collectively. While Americans believe that they 'run' America by the act of voting in a democracy, Mills adamantly disagreed stating that power was in fact in the hands of the aforementioned Power Elite.

**Practical Equilibrium.** In reference to George Homans' social exchange theory it is when the patterns of exchange become routinized and regular.

**Praxis.** Marx's belief that after people develop class consciousness, they must take action to overcome the "haves" and their economic system (i.e., capitalism).

**Predestination**. A belief that people were pre-selected by God for salvation or damnation.

**Predictability.** Building on George Ritzer's idea of the McDonaldization of society, predictability is the idea that the product that is being sold will be the same regardless of the place or time. Using McDonalds as an example, a Big Mac is the same at every McDonalds throughout the U.S.

**Prejudice.** An unfavorable, irrational, and rigid attitude that is generalized toward the members of a particular group.

**Premodern Societies.** Prior to the industrial revolution, there were four types of human societies: (1) hunting and gathering in which the group was nomadic, (2) pastoral in which groups were less nomadic and tied to a general area and were often headed by chieftains, (3) agrarian in which groups settled in a specific area, were usually headed by chieftains, and because they were no longer nomadic, inequalities first appeared, and (4) traditional societies which were primarily agrarian, headed by monarchs, and had even greater inequalities.

**Preparatory Stage.** George Herbert Mead (1863 – 1931) was a sociologist who is credited for being the creator of symbolic interactionism. Mead proposed that our "self" (i.e., self-awareness) was the result of social interaction. Mead believed that as children we pass through three stages as we develop our sense of self. The Preparatory Stage occurs by the age of two years, when children become able to mimic the behaviors of others in their social world even though they lack understanding what those behaviors mean. See also, George Herbert Mead.

**Prestige.** An intangible source of status that results from public recognition.

**Preventive Facework.** When we know that we are going to have to do or say something that may damage the way others think of us, we practice preventive facework. For instance, if you want others to think of you as competent, before asking for help on something you might say, "I wouldn't normally ask for help BUT..."

**Primary Deviance.** An initial act of deviance that may or may not result in a label being placed on the individual. If the initial act of deviance leads to the internalization of that deviant act, it can lead to secondary deviance which is where the individual may begin to accept the label which then leads to even greater deviance.

**Primacy Effect.** The tendency that when exposed to multiple speakers, to give more credence to the first speaker or information that was presented rather than the information provided by later speakers.

**Primary Group.** A group of people who share some common goals and who interact in the achievement of those goals on a regular basis constitute a group. Generally, groups can be divided into two types—primary and secondary. The characteristics of primary and secondary groups are:

- o   Primary group: face-to-face interactions occurring in small groups that

are socially intimate in nature and exist to accomplish goals through cooperation. Primary groups are informal in nature.
- o Secondary group: impersonal, formal in nature, and generally lacking social intimacy.

**Primary Socialization.** Highly influential socialization usually occurring in the home by immediate family members.

**Primogeniture.** Inheritance ritual where property of the estate is passed down to the oldest male in the family.

**Privatization.** The transfer of administration or outright ownership of businesses and organizations from government to privately owned organizations. The transition of a public company (i.e., listed on the stock market, has shareholders, and is publicly traded) to a private company that is owned by a smaller, non-public organization.

**Privilege.** The benefits and opportunities that come with status positions.

**Probability Sampling.** A probability sampling method uses some form of random selection. Random selection implies that every member of the population of study stands an equal chance of being selected for the sample.

**Processes of Socialization.** Socialization is the lifelong process by which people learn the do's and don'ts of the groups to which they belong through social interactions.

**Profession.** A profession is a paid occupation, based on a theoretical body of knowledge and expertise, requires specialized training or education, usually involves licensure, usually has a code of ethics, and is controlled by a governing body.

**Profit.** The belief according to social exchange theory that when rewards exceed costs, an actor will feel profited.

**Projection.** Projection involves the psychological process of projecting one's thoughts, feelings, and weaknesses on others to project one's self-esteem.

**Proletariat.** According to Marx, proletariat are the class of workers, especially industrial wage earners, who do not possess capital or property and must sell their labor to survive. He believed that after a middle class is pushed down to the lower class (the "have-nots") by the upper class ("the haves"), there will only be a two-class system.

**Propaganda.** Today in the U.S., propaganda is seen as misleading information designed to sway the public on some issue. The term has a negative connotation in U.S. society. However, during WWII, the Nazis considered propaganda as the official dissemination of government policy designed to make it easier for the German people to understand those policies. In fact, Joseph Goebbels' official title was Minister of Propaganda.

**Property.** In its broadest sense, a physical object that belongs to someone or something. Ownership is generally implied.

**Proposition.** A statement about how variables are related to each other or a specific component of a given theory. For instance, in Homans' social exchange theory, the first proposition is called the success proposition. The proposition suggests that when two people enter into a social interaction (all social interactions involve an exchange), actors in that interaction will later decide whether they have profited from that interaction by calculating whether their rewards have outweighed their costs. If rewards have indeed outweighed costs, the actor will conclude they profited. Thus, according to Homans, when actors feel as if they have profited they are more likely to repeat that interaction.

**Prosocial Behavior.** Prosocial behavior benefits other people in a given society and for which a reward is not expected. Generally, volunteering is seen as an example of prosocial behavior. Likewise, prosocial behavior is thought to be done for the sake of the greater good. Behavior towards another that is seen as altruistic or maybe even heroic.

**Prostitution.** Prostitutes sexually engage with clients for money. There are different types of prostitutes: street prostitutes, prostitutes who work in brothels—legal or illegal, and escorts. Today, sex trafficking is a new type of prostitution that forces young girls to engage in paid sex for the benefit of the trafficker.

**Protestant Work Ethic.** John Calvin (1509 – 1564) merged his theological ideas with those of Martin Luther (1483 – 1546), the father of Protestantism, to form a new religious ideology that led to new and radical attitudes about the value of work as it related to God. This new religious ideology, called Calvinism, purported that there were people chosen, blessed by God, and destined for Heaven, and these people were called the Elect (or sometimes referred to as the Elite). People who were not deemed as part of the Elect, according to Calvinism, were certainly bound for Hell and there was nothing they could do in this life to change that fact. But how could someone know if they were an Elect, and therefore bound for Heaven or Hell? Calvinism stressed that there were signs, found in daily life and deeds, that people could look for in order to determine who was an Elect and who was not. One of those signs was success. Success was measured by how well someone did in life by virtue of his or her physical efforts and attributes—active, pious, and hardworking. A person's wealth, legitimately earned through hard work, was therefore considered a sign that a person belonged to the Elect. People who were lazy, showed no ambition, and spent time in leisure activities rather than working, according to Calvinism, were damned. Calvin believed that all men should serve God through hard work, even the rich, because it was the will of God.

**Proximity Principle.** People who live near each other geographically, will be more likely to develop interpersonal relationships. This is true of friendships and dating. However, the Internet is changing the proximity principle to some degree.

**PSP.** Psychological social psychology. PSP research is almost always set in a laboratory and is strongly focused on the individual.

**Psychological Maltreatment.** Psychological abuse, also referred to as psychological violence, emotional abuse, or mental abuse is a legally recognized form of abuse. An abuser might subject their victim to psychological or emotional harm that could lead to psychological trauma such as anxiety disorders, depression, or PTSD (post-traumatic stress disorder). See also, Domestic Abuse.

**Psychological Femininity.** Someone who possesses stereotypical female characteristics or personality traits. Passiveness, nurturing, and compassionate would be examples of stereotypical female characteristics.

**Psychological Masculinity.** Someone who possesses stereotypical male characteristics or personality traits. Aggressiveness, rationality, impersonal would be examples of stereotypical male characteristics.

**Public Issues.** Problems people experience that are caused by social factors.

**Purdah.** The practice of keeping men from seeing women. Either women must cover their bodies (burqa and veil), walk behind men to show deference, eat only after men, and only speak when spoken to. Found mostly in Hindu and Muslim societies.

# Q - R

**Race.** A subjective classification of people into groups based on some physical characteristics. Anthropologists have shown that the term "race" is arbitrary in the way it is applied to groups and therefore lacks scientific meaning. However, race is still a social reality. People regularly identify others on the basis of appearance, pigeon-hole them into racial groups, and then treat them accordingly.

**Racism.** The belief that one group is superior to another based on certain physical characteristics that are subjectively referred to as "race." Individuals may be racists. When racism is the legal practice of a state, it is referred to as institutionalized racism. For instance, Southern states legally maintained and enforced segregation until the Civil Rights Act of 1964 was passed. Even though institutionalized racism technically ended in the 1960s, in a 2015 poll, 49% of Americans said that racism is a "big problem" in the U.S.

**Radical Feminism.** Theoretical framework which argues that gender inequality is rooted in the system of patriarchy itself and seeks to overthrow patriarchy and gender role in order to bring about gender equality.

**Radicalization.** Radicalization is a process by which an individual or group adopts extremist political, religious, or social ideas. While the motives of the particular political, religious, or social group may vary, two common themes are: (1) to undermine the status quo, and (2) reject mainstream ideas of equality, religious freedom, liberty, and tolerance.

**Random Sample.** Sometimes referred to as random selection. A sample drawn from a larger population so that everyone in the population of study as an equal chance of being selected. Random sampling leads researchers to be able to "generalize" their results on the sample to the population of study. See also, generalization.

**Range.** The spread of scores in a distribution. For instance, in looking at Rosenberg's Self-Esteem Scale, there are 10 scale items attempting to measure self-esteem collectively. For each scale item, respondents may choose one of four answers: strongly agree, agree, disagree, and strongly disagree. Rosenberg's scale is coded towards high self-esteem, so positive items are assigned a coded value of 3 whereas negative items are coded as 0. So, if someone were to choose the negative item for each of the 10 scale items, they would have a total score of 0, but if someone chose the positive item for each of the 10 scale items, they would have a score of 30. Therefore, the range of scores for the Rosenberg Self-Esteem Scale would be from 0 to 30. Marshall Rosenberg, above left.

**Rape.** A violent sexual act committed by someone, usually a male, on a female. Rape is considered to be a crime of violence, with domination and feelings of low self-worth as motivators for the perpetrator, and not as a sexual crime.

**Rape Myth.** The myth that women secretly enjoy sex forced on them. This is also associated with the archaic belief that women, because they were repressed and out of fear of being labeled, could not admit to enjoying sex, which led to a belief held by some men that "when a woman says no, she really meant yes."

**Rational-Legal Authority.** Based on Weber's theory of power, a system where authority comes from written rules and laws.

**Rationalization of Society.** Based on Weber's work on bureaucracies, the belief that bureaucracies would become the dominant system of power and use that power to control others and govern society as a whole.

**Realistic Group Conflict Theory.** A theory that suggests that conflict can develop between groups, usually lower-class groups, over scarce resources. Sometimes offered as a theory to explain prejudice between groups. This theory became a tenet of Allport's Theory of Contact where he suggested that when different groups can interact on a level playing field and the distribution of resources distributed equally, there would be a reduction in prejudice.

**Rebellion.** In anomie theory, a form of deviance that occurs when individuals reject culturally valued means and goals and substitute new means and goals. In political sociology, the expression of opposition to an established authority.

**Recency Effect.** The opposite of the primacy effect, the recency effect suggests that the last information received by an audience is given the most weight and influence.

**Recidivism.** Literally, repeat offending. When someone commits a crime, is convicted and sent to prison, and then after they are released recommits that crime or a similar crime, that is recidivism.

**Reciprocal Helping.** The belief that if someone helps another, that other person may someday return the help.

**Reciprocity Norm.** The expectation that if someone does a favor for another, the other person will return the favor at some later time.

**Reference Group.** The group of people to whom we compare ourselves because we identify with their values, beliefs, and behaviors. They also help define or evaluate beliefs, values, and behaviors.

**Reflexivity.** Associated with George Mead, reflexivity is the ability to put oneself in another person's place—to see things from the other person's perspective. Similar to the concept of empathy.

**Reform Movement.** A social movement that seeks social changes that are moderate as opposed to a revolution which seeks the total overthrow of the status quo.

**Regressive Movement.** A social movement that believes society was better off at an earlier time and seeks to restore that previous social order. For example, politicians will often speak of a return to family values of an earlier time, but in fact, never really existed.

**Relative Poverty.** There are two types of poverty measures: relative and absolute. A relative measure of poverty would examine how much any one person or household had in comparison to the average individuals or households had in that society. However, relative poverty might identify someone as poor with an income of $50,000 per year if the mean income for the community or society is $75,000 per year. Should someone making $50,000 per year be considered poor? What is needed is something that measures how much individuals and families need to survive and that is what an absolute measure of poverty does—it takes into account the costs of those things necessary for survival like food, shelter, medical costs, transportation costs, clothing, and other items. The condition of having too little income to buy the necessities-- food, shelter, clothing, and/or health care is called absolute poverty.

**Reliability (research).** Reliability is the degree a measure (e.g., an index or scale) produces consistent results as it is administered to different research groups over an extended period of time.

**Religion.** A set of shared beliefs and rituals among community members. According to Durkheim, these beliefs and rituals focus on the sacred and the supernatural. Durkheim reported that all religions had some major commonalities. Those commonalities are: (1) beliefs (which explain the unexplainable within a person's ability to understand), (2) the sacred (which are those things which inspire us with a sense of awe such as the cross or crucifix, holy beads, and holy water), (3) rituals and ceremonies (which are routinized behaviors that reinforce the faith and cohesiveness of the believers like chants, prayer, and genuflecting, (4) moral communities (which are communities of people who share the same beliefs and values), and (5) personal experience. Durkheim believed that members of a religion experience a personal relationship with the particular deity and that relationship can give purpose and meaning to people's lives.

**Religious Movement.** An organized religious group that rejects the values of the main religious body of which it is a part.

**Religiosity.** The degree to which a person is religious.

**Replication.** A methodological approach used to add reliability to a research study's findings. In other words, that if the study is conducted at a later time or with a different sample, the results should be the same.

**Representative Democracy.** A form of democracy in which the citizens do not vote on issues directly, but rather they elect representatives who will then vote on issues. Further, there are at least two political parties in a representative democracy.

**Requisite Needs.** The things that any system needs to function.

**Research Design.** The specific method used to conduct research. Research design includes how the sample will be selected and how the data will be measured and analyzed.

**Residential Segregation.** This occurs when people live in areas where there is a higher concentration of a certain race or ethnic group.

**Resocialization.** The process of de-socializing people from the norms and values of one group and then socializing them into the norms and values of another group.

**Resource Mobilization Theory.** The theory that stresses the importance of a social movement's ability to gather the financial resources they need to succeed.

**Response Cries.** Response cries are seemingly involuntary exclamations individuals make when they are taken by surprise, expressing pleasure, or in pain. They are not a reflex, but part of our controlled management of the details of social life.

**Retreatism.** In Merton's strain theory, retreatism is when people reject the institutionalized goals and the approved means to obtain those goals.

**Revictimization.** Research shows that adults who were abused as children have a slightly greater likelihood of abusing their own children. Further, adolescents who were abused as children have a greater likelihood of being abused.

**Revolution.** A complete rejection of the status quo by a powerful social movement and the subsequent restructuring of society.

**Revolutionary Movement.** A type of social movement whose objective is to replace the existing social structure with another.

**Riot.** An uncontrolled social reaction to some trigger. Riots are usually violent and destructive.

**Risky Shift.** Within groups people are more likely to take more risks than they would as individuals.

**Rites of Passage.** Formalized rituals among members of a community to acknowledge the transition from one status to another. Examples include a confirmation, bar mitzvah, or a wedding ceremony.

**Ritual.** In Durkheim's theory of religion, rituals are those things that bond members of a religion more closely together and reinforce the faith.

**Ritualism.** In Merton's Theory of Deviance, it is a form of quasi-deviance in which people obey norms outwardly by "going through the motions," but they lack inner commitment to their roles and the underlying values of the social system.

**Ritzer, George.** George Ritzer (right) is an American sociologist most notably known for his work on modern and postmodern sociological theory. Ritzer is also known for using Max Weber's ideas on rationalization to propose his concept of the McDonaldization of society—in which he believed that society adopted the principles and practices of the fast-food industry and in particular, McDonalds. Like McDonalds, Ritzer felt that society aimed to increase: (1) efficiency, (2) calculability, (3) predictability, and (4) control. See also, McDonaldization.

**Rival Hypothesis.** Simply a hypothesis that competes with another hypothesis when trying to investigate the same phenomenon.

**Role.** A set of expectations for people who occupy a given social position or status.

**Role Accumulation.** In our modern society with all the roles people need to act out, role accumulation refers to adding more roles and statuses to the those we already have. These additional roles can lead to role overload and role conflict.

**Role Conflict.** When people occupy statuses that may conflict with each other, roles may come into conflict.

**Role Exit.** As our statuses change, so do our roles. Role exit refers to leaving one status with its subsequent role expectations and occupying a new status which has different role expectations.

**Role Expectations.** Roles are expected normative behaviors when people occupy specific social statuses. For instance, being a college student is a status in our society, and therefore the expected normative behaviors expected for that role would include studying, attending lectures, and taking tests.

**Role Model.** Someone who is looked up to an admired and that others try to imitate.

**Role Overload.** When two or more social statuses compete with another for someone's time.

**Role Performance.** The particular action of a person as they perform a certain social role.

**Role Set.** As we occupy many statuses at the same time, we therefore expected to act out the appropriate roles for those statuses; together these statuses lead to a collection of roles that are referred to as a role set.

**Role Strain.** Conflicting expectations within the same role.

**Rowdyism.** "Soccer hooligans" are an example of rowdyism. Rowdyism refers to unacceptable behavior, like interpersonal violence, that occurs as a result of social interactions during spectator events. See also, soccer hooligans.

**Ruling Class.** Marx would refer to the ruling class as either the Bourgeoisie, owners, or haves. The ruling class owns the means of production and therefore has power with which they use to rule a society—directly or indirectly through shared ideals with other members of the ruling class. See also, C. Wright Mills the Power Elite.

**Ruling Class Ideology.** Building on the idea that the masses are manipulated and exploited by the elite, it is the belief that the elite present a false view of society in order to secure their position of authority and control.

**Rumor.** Research has found that people have a need to fear the worst, to provide information that may scare others to action, and to vilify another person or institution. Rumors, usually lacking fact or substance, are usually passed informally from one person to another.

**Sample Survey.** A survey is a research method used to collect data from a research sample.

**Sampling.** Social research is almost always concerned about specific populations of people—for example, people in the U.S. 65 years of age and older. However, if I were to attempt to survey all Americans 65 years of age and older, I would need to survey almost 50 million people. As you can imagine, that would take a great deal of money and time. So, instead I would probably decide to use a smaller sample instead. Sampling is the process of selecting people from a research population so that by studying the sample we may generalize our results back to the population from which they were chosen.

The logic of sampling is that if the sample is drawn randomly from the research population (i.e., the population we wish to study), everyone in the population has an equal chance of being selected for the sample. If that's the case, the random sample we drew should mirror the characteristics of the research population being studied. So, let's say I know that the average annual income of elderly in the U.S. is $25,000 per year, I should expect to see that same average income, or close to it, in my randomly drawn sample. Additionally, maybe I also know that the average of Americans 65 years and older is 75.1 years and I find that the average age of my sample members is about the same, let's say 75.2 years of age. If that's true, we can say the sample mirrors the characteristics of the research population. That allows us to say that what is true of the sample, is also true of the population.

So, once we have drawn our random sample, we perform our research using that sample. When we get done with our research on our sample, and reach some conclusions based on the data we have collected from them, we are ready to generalize our results from the sample to our research population. In other words, if that sample was randomly drawn from our research population, the sample should mirror the characteristics of the research population, which then allows us to say that if the sample mirrors the characteristics of our research population, the sample should mirror the characteristics of our research population—this allows us to say that whatever research findings we discovered for our sample, they should be true for the population as well. See also, generalization.

**Sanction.** Generally, sanctions are punishments designed to informally or formally bring a person back into compliance with mainstream beliefs, values, and laws. For instance, sanctions would be applied to someone convicted of robbing a bank (going to jail), a professional female golfer (labeled as lesbian), or a little girl who likes to climb trees (called a tomboy).

**Scale.** A scale is a type of composite measure that is composed of several items that are logically related to one another and is used to extract data on a relatively complex variable or phenomenon. For instance, depression is a relatively complex phenomenon to measure. You can't ask just one question about some issue related to depression and expect to know just how depressed someone really is. You need a scale to do so because there are a number of factors that are needed to adequately assess self-esteem.

The most commonly used scale is the Likert scale, which contains response categories such as "strongly agree," "agree," "disagree," and "strongly disagree." For instance, we are interested in measuring self-esteem. The following is the Rosenberg Self-Esteem Scale (1965):

1. On the whole I am satisfied with myself.
   Strongly Agree  Agree  Disagree  Strongly Disagree
       3         2        1         0

2. At times I think that I am no good at all.
   Strongly Agree  Agree  Disagree  Strongly Disagree
       0         1        2         3

3. I feel that I have a number of good qualities.
   Strongly Agree  Agree  Disagree  Strongly Disagree
       3         2        1         0

4. I am able to do things as well as most other people.
   Strongly Agree  Agree  Disagree  Strongly Disagree
       3         2        1         0

5. I feel I do not have much to be proud of.
   Strongly Agree  Agree  Disagree  Strongly Disagree
       0         1        2         3

6. I certainly feel useless at times.
   Strongly Agree  Agree  Disagree  Strongly Disagree
       0         1        2         3

7. I feel that I am a person of worth, at least the equal of others.

Strongly Agree  Agree  Disagree  Strongly Disagree
       3          2        1              0

8. I wish I could have more respect for myself.
Strongly Agree  Agree  Disagree  Strongly Disagree
       0          1        2              3

9. All in all, I am inclined to feel that I am a failure.
Strongly Agree  Agree  Disagree  Strongly Disagree
       0          1        2              3

10. I take a positive attitude toward myself.
Strongly Agree  Agree  Disagree  Strongly Disagree
       3          2        1              0

For a scale, each response is coded with a number—the higher the number for each scale item, the more it is associated with high self-esteem. Therefore, if we code the items, and we coded towards high self-esteem, and we coded from 0 to 3, the range of possible scores for this scale would be 0 (for those who always chose the response associated with low self-esteem) to 30 (for those who always chose the response associated with high self-esteem). Therefore, the higher the score, the higher the self-esteem.

**Scapegoating.** Blaming a target group for the hardship a particular group is experiencing. For instance, the Nazis, and many other Germans as well, blamed the Jews and Communists for the German nation's surrender at the end of World War I. Because of the widespread use of this scapegoating, Jews, Communists, and other groups were targeted by the Nazis which then led to the taking away of their rights, and eventually, to their mass murder.

**Schemas.** Cognitive structures about objects or groups of people which guide people in their interactions with that particular object or group and the acceptance of new information into the already formed schema. Is often associated with prejudice. Once someone develops a schema of someone perceived as different from them, future information resulting from interactions with people from that particular outgroup will be selectively attended to so that the new information conforms to the already developed schema a person has of that outgroup.

**Science.** Science uses the scientific method, strictly defined rules and procedures, to obtain facts about some phenomenon.

**Scientific Management.** The belief that breaking down tasks into smaller tasks leads to increased overall productivity. See also, Taylorism.

**Scientific Productivity.** Building a body of knowledge for a particular scientific field of study. Collecting facts using the scientific method, the sciences then use those facts to confirm or disconfirm hypotheses and theories. If those facts support hypotheses and theories, results are then published which furthers the body of knowledge in that scientific discipline. As other researchers come along who want to investigate related phenomenon, previously published research (which makes up that body of knowledge within that scientific field), is used to provide a foundation for this new research.

**Scientific Revolution.** Replacing one scientific theory with another more advanced theory.

**Scripts.** Scripts provide an understanding of specific situations even though an actor may not have experienced the situation beforehand. Though not usually appearing formally as a book with written instructions, these scripts tell us how to act or what to expect in novel situations. For instance, because you have watched television ads for ocean cruises, know people who talk about the cruises they have taken, watched movies set on ocean cruises, and read stories and reviews about ocean cruises, you have some expectations about what an ocean cruise would be like. Therefore, you also know what kind of behaviors are expected on a cruise, even though you've never been on one. Scripts help us prepare for these novel situations.

**Second Shift.** The "second shift" refers to women coming home after working full-time in paid labor only to have to start their second shift by assuming household responsibilities (e.g., cooking, cleaning, childcare, etc.).

**Secondary Analysis.** A type of research method that uses already obtained data.

**Secondary Deviance.** Primary deviance is when society makes something of a behavior—in other words, an act that is considered deviant in some way. Secondary deviance occurs when the actor who has committed a primary act of deviance internalizes and accepts the deviant label that society puts on them. See also, self-fulfilling prophecy.

**Secondary Economic Sector.** The part of the economy responsible for turning raw resources into finished products.

**Secondary Group.** A group with formal ties between members that exists to accomplish specific tasks. Generally, groups can be divided into two types—primary and secondary. The characteristics of primary and secondary groups are:

- Primary group: face-to-face interactions occurring in small groups that are socially intimate in nature and exist to accomplish goals through cooperation. Primary groups are informal in nature.
- Secondary group: impersonal, formal in nature, and generally lacking social intimacy.

**Secondary Socialization.** Socialization that usually occurs outside of the home and later in life.

**Sect.** A group of people with different religious beliefs, maybe even considered heretical, from those of the parent religious body. Sects therefore pull away from the established parent religious body and establish its own religious body. Generally, sects are small in nature when compared to the parent religion, and have a structure that is not as well organized (especially in the beginning) as that of the parent religious body. This schism usually results from hotly debated religious doctrines associated with the belief system of the parent religious body. Sects are seen as standing apart from mainstream religion. Examples include the Amish, Mennonites, Quakers, and Shakers.

**Secure Attachment Style.** Largely and initially formed during childhood, it is characterized by secure attachments to others, which are displayed as trust, a feeling of being valued, and a lack of fear being abandoned.

**Secularization.** Refers to the historical process in which religion loses social and cultural significance. As a result of secularization, the role of religion in modern societies becomes restricted.

**Segregation.** The physical separation of a minority group from the dominant group. Examples include African Americans between 1865 and 1965, and South African blacks under Apartheid.

**Self.** Mead proposed that our "self" (i.e., self-awareness) was the result of social interaction. Mead believed that as children we pass through three stages as we develop our sense of self. Those three stages are:

- **Preparatory Stage:** By the age of two years, children are able to mimic the behaviors of others in their social world even though they lack understanding what those behaviors mean.
- **Play Stage:** Between the ages of two and six years, children began to role-play which then allows them to take on the roles of important people in their social world.
- **Game Stage:** By the age of seven years and older, children have learned what their role is in their social world while they continue to be able to take on the roles of others as if in a game.

**Self-Affirmation Theory.** A theory that attempts to explain how people deal with negative information that might influence their self-concept. Sometimes people will only seek out information that confirms their sense of self, and sometimes they seek to find information that maximizes their sense of self in other areas as a way of compensating.

**Self-Awareness.** The ability for introspection--though often flawed and biased.

**Self-Concept.** A collection of beliefs about who you see yourself as being.

**Self-Consciousness.** Self-consciousness is the process by which people become self-aware. Self-awareness is when people are aware that they are being evaluated by others and are therefore the subject of attention by those others. In Goffman's terms, it is the awareness that they are on-stage and their performance scrutinized by others.

**Self-Disclosure.** The act of being candid with others and revealing innermost personal information.

**Self-Discrepancies.** The difference of how we are perceived by others and how we would want to be perceived by others. In Goffman's view this would be judged as the inability for an individual to successfully manage their impression when on-stage.

**Self-Esteem.** The overall evaluation we have of our self-worth.

**Self-Esteem Motive.** Motivational efforts to preserve and protect one's self-esteem. People often develop opinions supported by their reference groups because this leads to preserved or enhanced self-esteem. Likewise, people tend to affiliate themselves with groups who are part of valued groups and to shy away from groups who are seen as lesser valued groups.

**Self-Fulfilling Prophecy.** Largely stemming from labeling theory, when society believes something negative or deviant about someone, they predict that person will continue on that path of deviance, but by doing so society sets up a situation that influences that person in such a way that the belief or prediction comes true.

**Self-Handicapping.** Activities in which people work to limit their abilities so that they can fault those inabilities for their failure to perform some task.

**Semi-Peripheral Nations.** Middle-income nations that are undergoing the process of modernization and who often exploit the poorer nations as well.

**Serial Monogamy.** Several successive, short-term marriages over the course of a lifetime.

**Self-Perception Theory.** The belief that our behaviors provide us with insight into our own thoughts and attitudes.

**Self-Regulation.** The process by which people intentionally control their actions either to limit cognitive dissonance, project a positive image to others (i.e., manage their impressions), or to avoid sanctions.

**Self-Schemas.** The many self-attributes one has of him or herself that together form a person's self-concept.

**Self-Serving Bias.** The mental process by which we see our positive inner mental forces at work as leading to our successes but to see outer, environmental or situational factors at work when we experience failure. See also, locus of control.

**Self-Verification.** In order to find support for our self-concept, this is the process by which we find examples of our successes as added proof to our positive self-concept.

**Serial monogamy.** A process whereby individuals marry more than one person in the course of their lifetime. Each new marriage, however, follows the end of the previous one.

**Sex.** The result of biological distinctions between males and females as opposed to gender which is socially constructed (i.e., the expected roles males and females occupy because of their sex).

**Sexism.** The belief that one sex is superior to the other.

**Sexual Harassment.** Verbal, physical, or emotional sexual acts or comments that make someone feel uncomfortable or threatened in some social arena. While often associated with the workplace, sexual harassment can occur in virtually every social environment.

**Sexuality.** The attitudes, norms, and emotions associated culturally with one's sex drive.

**Shamans**. The individual in a preliterate tribe who attempts to heal group members by calling upon spirits to help control or heal diseases.

**Sibling.** A brother or sister.

**Significant Other.** Cooley's belief that there are people in our lives whose opinion of us and our actions is so important to us that they influence our thoughts and actions. Also, a colloquial phrase to refer to a husband, wife, boyfriend or girlfriend.

**Simmel, Georg.** Georg Simmel (1858 – 1918) (right) was a German sociologist who is known for his work on groups and group processes. Among many of Simmel's notable contributions to the field of sociology was the idea that the fastest and most effective way to increase the cohesiveness of a group was to impose an external threat--real or imagined.

**Single-Headed Household.** The most common type of alternative family in the U.S. today.

**Skilled Worker.** Someone who has significant and valuable skills put to use in the workforce.

**Slavery.** Extreme form of inequality in which certain people own other people as property and use them as a source of labor.

**Smelser, Neil.** Neil Smelser (b. 1930) is known for his work on collective behavior. He is most known for his strain theory (also known as value added theory). Smelser believed there were six elements necessary for people to engage in collective behavior:

- Structural conduciveness. Situations or factors that allow for particular behaviors to occur.
- Structural strain. There must be some force or change in society that produces a strain toward further change.
- Generalized belief. At some point the group becomes aware of the problem and of itself as a group force.
- Precipitating factors. There is some kind of occurrence that triggers action.
- Mobilization for action. People solidify their group efforts and become organized.
- Failure of social control. Do authorities respond to the new social

movement or do they ignore it? If they ignore it, there is a failure of social control and the movement is allowed to grow and produce societal wide change.

**Smith, Dorothy.** Dorothy Smith (1926 - present) is a Canadian sociologist known for her work on feminist sociology, including race, class, and gender within her Feminist Standpoint theory.

**Social aggregate**. A collection of people who find themselves gathered together at a particular time and location but who do not interact or share a common sense of identity. An example would be a group of people waiting for a train.

**Social Anxiety.** A distressing emotion that someone may feel as an outcome of an interpersonal interaction that conflicts with one's own image of themselves. See also, impression management.

**Social Capital.** Social networks have the potential to provide useful information, influential social ties, a basis for power of some kind (e.g., political and organizational), and reciprocity in social exchanges. Social capital is largely built on social networks. Therefore, networking skills are essential to increased social capital. Social capital can be increased by the use of these social networks by reciprocity and equitable treatment of those in the network and by trusting those in the network to add to a network member's social capital when it is legitimately due. People with large social networks, and a high degree of social capital, usually have substantial "people skills." Often times these people skills will involve the use of ingratiation, flattery, and small talk establishing commonalities between network members.

**Social Categorization.** The mental process of putting people into rigid categories based on a few attributes. Often associated with prejudice.

**Social Change.** The transformation in the way society is organized, its values, beliefs, or norms. For example, by giving women the right to vote in the 19th Amendment to the Constitution, the result was dramatic cultural change. Another example would be the U.S. Supreme Court's decision that state marriage laws that prohibited same-sex marriage were unlawful has changed the cultural acceptance of gays and lesbians as having equal rights, is in the process of allowing the term "family" to be applied to them, changing employee benefit packages, and many other normative practices.

**Social channeling**. A social conflict theory describing how upper class parents prepare their children for positions of wealth and power.

**Social Class.** A group's position in a social hierarchy based on status, occupational prestige, wealth, and education.

**Social Cognition.** A social psychological process that examines how people not only process, store, and apply information in their daily lives, but also how it affects social interactions. In psychology, cognition is the process of thinking and reasoning.

**Social Comparison Theory.** A theory that suggests we form our self-concept, in particular our thoughts and actions, by comparing ourselves to others.

**Social Control.** Social control mechanisms are actions taken by society to prevent deviance (and crime). Those mechanisms include socialization, religion, informal sanctions for minor violations (e.g., scolding, ridicule, laughter, gossip) of normative behaviors, and formal sanctions for major violations of normative behaviors (i.e., violations of the law).

**Social Construction of Reality.** Building on symbolic interactionism, humans build social reality by consensus. If a group or a larger society interprets and defines situations in the same way, they have socially constructed reality. While bricks, flooring, toilets, and automobiles may all be real in their physical form, social reality only exists when humans create it by their shared agreement as to what that social reality is.

**Social Control Theory (social bond theory).** Based on Travis Hirschi's book *Causes of Delinquency* (1969), Hirschi (1935 – present) (right) proposed that social bonds play a large part in encouraging conformity through the socialization process and inhibiting deviance—especially criminal deviance. He identified those bonds as: (1) attachments (to the group to which the person belongs), (2) investments (e.g., financial resources, higher education), (3) involvements (i.e., being active and engaged in the community), and (4)  beliefs (i.e., religious values, knowing something is a violation of the law). He also believed that the strength of these four elements would contribute to whether they prevented deviance; the stronger the elements, the less likely someone will deviate from social norms and commit crime. While primarily developed to explain juvenile delinquency, Hirschi's theory has been expanded to include crime among all ages.

**Social Darwinism.** A belief system that advocates survival of the fittest.

**Social Distance.** How close we feel to other people.

**Social Exchange Theory.** Homans' social exchange theory suggests that we are in a constant state of social exchanges with others. Based on economic theory, exchange theory suggests that when we profit from a social exchange, we will most likely repeat it, but if we don't profit, we will most likely not repeat the exchange. Homans' social exchange theory has 13 propositions that attempt to explain exchange relationships. Different from the economic model of exchange, social exchange theory makes predictions about the interactions between actors engaged in exchanges. Social exchange theory, which is a macro theory, can be used at the micro level to study romantic relationships, domestic abuse, and family dynamics. See also, Exchange Theory.

**Social Facilitation.** Developed by Floyd Allport, an American psychologist (1890-1979), is the process by which humans modify their behavior depending on the presence of others.

**Social Facts.** Social moral structures that are external to and coercive of the individual; they have a fact-like basis in that they are difficult to resist.

**Social Forces.** The unseen forces of social structures on people and culture that are real in their consequences.

**Social Group.** Two or more people in an interaction and who share some commonalities.

**Social Identities.** The idea that our self-concept is largely influenced by the groups to which we belong.

**Social Inequality.** The existence of unequal opportunities for people within a society and which is based on features such as sex, race, ethnicity, religion, sexual orientation, disability, and more.

**Social Influences.** As humans relating to one another through social interactions and within social institutions, we are influenced by social and cultural ideas and normative practices. That influence has the potential for a dramatic effect on our behavior. Social processes that are affected by social influences include socialization, social change, and conformity.

**Social Institutions.** Socially constructed patterns of interaction at the societal level. Examples of social institutions include the family, government, the educational system, and religion.

**Social Integration.** Refers to the level of cohesiveness within a society; the intensity of the bonds felt between people of the same society.

**Social Interaction.** Experiences in which people relate with one another through the use of symbols. There are five types of social interaction: exchange, collaboration, competition, conflict, and coercion. See also, channels of communication.

**Socialism.** Social, political, and economic systems where the people own the means of production, property is communal and not privately owned, the government controls the economy, and the good of the many outweighs the good of the few.

**Socialist Societies.** Economic systems in which the state owns the means of production. See also, socialism.

**Socialization.** The lifelong process by which people learn the do's and don'ts of the groups to which they belong.

**Social Loafing.** When working in large tasks groups, individual activity may be less scrutinized and therefore some group members may be less productive and depend on others to pick up the slack.

**Social Mobility.** The movement of an individual to another social or status group.

**Social Movements.** Collective action with the intent to replace the existing social order with a new one.

**Social Networks.** The links formed between individuals, families, cliques, and other groups.

**Social Norm.** Role expectations for people occupying a status. See, norms.

**Social Penetration Theory.** A theory that proposes the more people self-disclose to others, who in return do the same, that relationship is strengthened. This ties into the idea that people tend to like people who like them.

**Social Perception.** The process by which we attempt to understand other persons and their actions.

**Social Power.** See, power.

**Social Learning Theory.** A theory that suggests humans learn behaviors through observation and imitation and that those behaviors are rewarded or reinforced.

**Social Mobility.** Social mobility refers to movement between classes in a class system. There are two methods used to measure social mobility.

- A vertical change of social status within the same generation. We can measure where a person is in terms of their class position and then measure where they are in terms of class position at some later time in their life. If there is a difference in class position between those two periods, we can say that there is evidence of mobility of class positions.
- A vertical change of social status from one generation to the next. We can measure where a person is in terms of their class position and then measure where their parents are in terms of their class position. If there is a difference in class position between them and their parents, then we can say that there is evidence of mobility of class positions.

**Social Movement.** A group that seeks social changes within their society.

**Social Network.** A social network is made up of both strong and weak ties. Strong ties would be those people who have direct and supportive links to all persons in the particular social network, while weak ties refer to members of a social network who have ties with people outside the network, but those ties assist others in the network in some way—for instance, with information. A social network is a social structure in which ongoing social interactions between members occur.

**Social Psychology.** Social psychology is that point of intersection between sociology and psychology. As a discipline, social psychology studies the effects of the social environment on individual behavior. In sociology, social psychology, also known as sociological social psychology, socio-psychology, or psychological sociology, is an area of sociology that focuses on the interrelations of the environment and biological predispositions (e.g., personality, cognition). The primary research methods for social psychology include surveys and experiments.

**Social Reflexivity.** People consciously thinking about their many interactions in a given time-frame and assessing their actions as either being appropriate or inappropriate. Akin to their self-awareness of a social conscience.

**Social Reproduction.** Refers to how societies reproduce themselves from one generation to the next.

**Social Research Process.** The seven steps of the sociological research process are:

- Defining the research problem
- Reviewing the evidence
- Making the problem precise
- Working out a design
- Carrying out the research
- Interpreting the results
- Reporting the findings

**Social Role.** Behaviors that are expected from people occupying specific roles in society. See also, norms.

**Social Role Theory.** At any given time, people hold different statuses. Each of those statuses carries with it normative role expectations. The carrying out of those varied roles are performed within cultural expectations. For instance, being a mother is a status and therefore carries with it a number of different roles. Those roles include being caring, nurturing, cooking, diaper changer, soother, teacher, and a good mother. In this example, women know how society expects them to carry out those roles and try to do so in order to conform, not be stigmatized in the event of not carrying out a particular role as society expects, or in a worst-case scenario, goes to jail for a severe violation of the associated normative behavior for a specific role. Women know that it is not acceptable to leave a child in a hot car during the summer, and they know if they did so they would be heavily sanctioned.

**Social Sciences.** Disciplines that study human behavior in some way. In addition to sociology, the social sciences generally include psychology, anthropology, economics, political science.

**Social Stratification.** Social stratification, or often referred to as social inequality, exists when there is an unequal division of resources. These resources, or socioeconomic factors, include power, which can come from wealth or the political institution, class, and status. Stratification refers to the "layers" on a hierarchy and where one falls on that hierarchy. In Marx's theory of stratification, he proposed that there were at the time of his writings, three noteworthy classes: (1) the "haves," or the owners of the means of production, (2) a middle class of doctors and merchants, and (3) the "have-nots," or those that worked for the "haves."

Systems of stratification, or social inequality, have evolved over time as mankind went from hunting and gathering to pastoral and then agrarian societies. In agrarian societies man stayed in one place, rather than being nomadic. Pastoral societies were only slightly less nomadic that agrarian societies in that they tended not to move great distances to find areas more suitable for the grazing of their livestock. Marx believed that both agrarian and pastoral societies were essentially without stratification as all tribal or clan members pretty well had the same possessions, as they were a liability when moving from one area to the next.

**Social Structure.** Recurrent and patterned relationships that become "real" as they are socially constructed. Social structure only exists when there is consensus on how to define it.

**Social Structure and Personality.** A sociological social psychological perspective that focuses on the interactions between the individual and larger societal conditions.

**Society.** People who live within a geographical territory that is clearly divided and distinct from surrounding societies, share dominant cultural values, share some degree of nationalistic unity. Generally, countries can be considered societies.

**Sociobiology.** The study of human behavior resulting from or being influenced by biology.

**Socioeconomic Status (SES).** An individual's socioeconomic status results from their occupational status, higher education, income, and wealth.

**Sociology.** The study of groups and how they influence people and how people influence and shape groups; the study of humans in social interaction.

**Sociological Imagination.** The ability to see personal issues within the larger social context. For instance, many people see divorce as a personal problem but there are many social factors that influence divorce and also influenced by divorce. See also, C. Wright Mills.

**Sociological Theory.** Theory is used by all sciences to study particular phenomena. Sociological theory allows sociologists to systematically gather facts about our social world, which then allow them to explain that social world, and then with that understanding, theory allows sociologists to predict future outcomes in that social world.

**Somatosensory Pleasure.** The ability of non-sexual touch to affect pleasure. Research has found that societies high in somatosensory pleasure (i.e., touchy-feeliness), score low in approval of violence, which societies found to be low in somatosensory pleasure tend to score high in approval of violence.

**Sovereignty.** The legitimate authority a government has over a specific territory and the people within that territory.

**Spuriousness.** There are two conditions where there may appear to be an association between an independent and dependent variable but in fact doesn't provide useful data. The first is where there is an accidental association between the independent and dependent variables and that would not occur should the research be repeated elsewhere. In other words, the results are due to sheer luck. The second type of spuriousness is where there is really a third variable involved and that variable is the true independent variable. The classic example is where it has been proven there is an association between the number of fire trucks at the scene of a fire (i.e., the independent variable) and the amount of fire damage (i.e., the dependent variable). But in reality, the true independent variable is size of the fire and both the number of fire trucks at the scene and the amount of fire damage are dependent variables.

**SSP.** Sociological social psychology. Usually involves non-laboratory research with a focus on group behavior rather than individual behavior.

**Stage Theory.** A theory suggesting that all nations develop in stages over an extended period of time.

**Stalking.** Stalking is a pattern of behavior that makes someone feel afraid, nervous, harassed, or in danger. Contrary to popular belief, stalking does not necessarily mean someone is physically trailing a victim.

**State.** The highest institutionalized and legitimate political order within a given territory.

**State Terrorism.** A state using illegitimate methods (e.g., torture, death squads, kidnapping) to eliminate political threats by its citizens.

**Status.** A socially defined position in society that carries with it certain prescribed rights, obligations, and expected behaviors. Statuses may either be ascribed or achieved. Ascribed status is a social position assigned to a person by society without regard for the person's unique talents or characteristics. Achieved status is a social position that is within our power to change.

**Status-Attainment Model.** The idea that parental education and occupation as well as their child's education and occupation largely effect the child's status as an adult.

**Status Group.** A shared social identity based on similar values and lifestyles.

**Status Inconsistency.** Status inconsistency may occur when someone holds at least two statuses that are unequal in their value to society. For instance, an African-American who is president of the U.S. Being the president of the U.S. carries extremely high status, but we live in a society that tends to award lesser status to African-Americans.

**Status quo.** A term used to describe that which currently exists. In a sociological sense, it generally applies to maintaining or changing the existing social structure and values.

**Status Set.** The entirety of all the statuses that we hold at any given point.

**Status Symbol.** Material goods or activities that when possessed are thought to display one's social standing or prestige to others.

**Steps of (general) Science.** The steps of science, or the scientific method, are those steps and processes used in science to discover and collect facts about our world. Ultimately, the collection of these facts tell us something about our world and may result in our ability to predict outcomes.

- **Step 1: We first <u>perceive a phenomenon</u>** or phenomena (things we have not yet labeled or named).
- **Step 2: We <u>conceptualize</u>** (we name the phenomenon or phenomena).
- **Step 3: We <u>hypothesize</u>** (we construct a hypothetical cause and effect relationship between two or more concepts).
- **Step 4: We <u>arrive at a fact</u>.** After testing empirically (i.e., scientifically by experiment or study) we attempt to verify our hypothesis.
- **Step 5: We now <u>construct a theory</u>.** After testing and retesting our hypotheses many times, and collecting facts that support our hypothesis, we now attempt to put them together and construct a theory.
- **Step 6: If we empirically verify our theory, we have a scientific law.**

**Steps in the Social Research Process**

- **Step 1: Define the Problem.** What is the particular problem you wish to investigate? The more specific you are, the more definitive will be your research results.
- **Step 2: Review the Literature.** The next step is to review the existing literature related to the problem you wish to study. Prior research findings may influence your research methodology. The last step in the research process is to publish research findings. By publishing research findings there is potential for those findings to serve as a

foundation for future research on a related topic. This is how the body of knowledge in each scientific field is increased.
- **Step 3: State your Hypothesis.** A hypothesis is a testable statement between two or more variables. Hypotheses are formulated from previous research. In other words, there must be a scientific basis for a hypothesis.
- **Step 4: Identify the Research Design.** After formalizing the hypothesis, researchers must then decide what research method would be best in order to collect the information necessary to prove the hypothesis. Questions to be dealt with at this point include: (1) how will the variable or variables be measured? (2) how will the research sample be selected from the research population? (3) what type of statistical analysis will be used (if it is a quantitative study)?
- **Step 5: Collect the Data.** There are a number of research tools that can used to gather information. For instance, surveys, experiments, interviews, participant observation, or content analysis.
- **Step 6: Analyze the Data.** Using the appropriate data analysis tool, analyzing the data will tell researchers if their hypothesis is supported or not.
- **Step 7: Report your Findings.** Researchers need to publish their findings as this potentially provides the basis for future research.
- **Step 8: State your Conclusions and Introduce a Discussion.** Drawing conclusions involves trying to answer your specific research questions. For instance, was your research question supported? If not, why not? What limitations in the study should be considered in evaluating the results? Does your research findings suggest directions for future research on the same topic? Were there methodological issues with your research that might be important for future research?

**Stereotype.** Stereotypes are generalizations about types or groups of people based on relatively weak experiences or knowledge. In other words, it is easier to form stereotypes about groups of people with whom we have little personal or face-to-face experience. This results in people exaggerating negative aspects of those about whom they form stereotypes. Likewise, once a stereotype is formed, research has found that people tend to selectively attend to information that supports their stereotypes and ignore information that challenges their stereotypes.

A cognitive source of prejudice, categorization involves the way that people categorize or organize the world. Research has found that it can be easy and quick for people to use stereotypes when: (1) they are pressed for time (Kaplan et al., 1993), (2) preoccupied (Gilbert & Hixon, 1991), (3) tired (Bodenhausen, 1990), (4) emotionally aroused (Esses et al., 1993), and (5) when they are too young to appreciate diversity (Biernat, 1991).

**Stereotype Threat.** A condition when any action of a stereotypical group member might fit that stereotype and thus perpetuate the stereotype and provide further "evidence" of the stereotype by those that are prejudiced against that stereotypical group.

**Stigma.** A negative label attached to some action or group.

**Stigmatization.** The process of applying a damaging label to someone with the intent of eliminating their deviance and bringing them back into the fold (i.e., to conform to normative beliefs and practices).

**Strain Theory.** Robert K. Merton (1910 – 2003) (right) was an American sociologist who believed that we are all taught by our shared culture to want the same cultural goals, but he argued that some people feel that they don't have access to those goals using legitimate and approved means...such as going to college or experience. Some people he said use inappropriate and illegitimate means to get those cultural goals. Merton identified five modes of adaptation:

- Conformists who accepted the cultural goals and the institutionalized means to obtain those goals.
- Innovators who accepted the cultural goals but used non-institutionalized means to obtain those goals.
- Ritualists who rejected the cultural goals but accepted the institutionalized means.
- Retreatists who rejected the cultural goals and the institutionalized means to obtain goals.
- Rebel who may or may not accept the cultural goals and who may or may not accept the institutionalized means to obtain the goals.

**Strategic Self Presentation.** See also, Self-Presentation and Impression Management.

**Stratification.** A social and economic system based on a hierarchy of wealth and privilege. A highly stratified system as a hugely unequal division of wealth and property. Marx's work suggests that this unequal division of wealth and power leads to conflict over available resources. See also, conflict perspective.

**Structural-Functional Perspective.** A dominant theoretical perspective in sociology proposed by Talcott Parsons (1902 – 1979). Parsons published his seminal work on a general theory of action in *Towards a General Theory of Action*. Parson thought of his general theory of action as being applicable to all social behavior throughout history. Though Parsons thought referring to his theoretical ideas as structural functionalism was too simplistic, he was however responsible for bringing Max Weber's work to the U.S.

In looking at society as a system, and with survival and equilibrium as crucial for the system, Parsons believed there were four important components necessary to fulfil those goals: (1) social systems must adapt to changes in their environment or die; (2) systems must have clearly stated goals; (3) elements of the system must work together and work within the overarching greater system; and (4) the system must maintain norms and values which justify the actions within the system.

**Subculture.** Every society has a dominant culture, and in heterogeneous societies, there are also subcultures. Subcultures accept the dominant culture's overall values, but have their own values, beliefs, language, and norms additionally. Examples of subcultures includes Italian Americans, African-Americans, Jewish Americans, Asian Americans, Latinos and Hispanics.

**Subjective Meanings.** Symbolic interpretations, or meaning, varies from one person to the next at a lower and more personal level. At a higher level, societies should have few if any subjective meanings because reality is socially constructed through consensus, but at lower levels (e.g., in one on one interactions) consensus may not be applicable and the situation misunderstood because of this subjectivity. For instance, John and Mary are good friends in college—in fact, Mary has a crush on John. Soon after graduating college, John moves away. Mary is devastated, but gets on with her life. One day John calls Mary, tells her that he will be in town for the weekend, and asks her if she wants to go out. Mary is ecstatic. In preparation for John's arrival, Mary goes out and buys a new dress, has her hair and nails done, and buys expensive perfume to help set the mood. At the appointed time, the doorbell rings. With a smile from ear to ear, Mary opens the door only to discover John and two of his friends standing there. "Are you ready to go out?" asks John. As the smile disappears from Mary's face, she realizes she has misinterpreted John's request to "go out."

**Subjective Social Class.** Most Americans identify themselves as members of the middle class, but for many of those people, and depending on the arbitrary method used to assign class positions, many are not classified as members of the middle class, but rather as members of the lower class. Therefore, people subjectively think of themselves as belonging to one class or another, but that view may not be shared by others.

**Subliminal Perception.** The sub-conscious processing of information that influences a person's attitudes or behaviors without that person being aware of those sub-conscious attitudes. The use of subliminal messaging can be traced back to the ancient Greeks, but it is still alive all around us. For instance, imagine a fast-food commercial. All messages directed at people have two components: that which is spoken and that which is subliminally projected. In a fast-food commercial you may hear the spokesperson talk about their children's meal, or the sale price on a particular item, but while you hear those spoken messages you are seeing happy, healthy, non-overweight people enjoying the food. The subliminal message sent to our brain is that I can eat fast-food and stay trim and healthy, which any reasonably intelligent person knows simply isn't true.

**Suburb.** Created in the 1950s, suburbs served as an alternative to city life, which was especially popular with couples raising children. The term "urban sprawl" refers to widespread creation of suburbs outside of urban areas throughout the U.S.

**Sunbelt.** An area south of the 37th parallel in the U.S. which draws people of all ages, but especially the elderly from colder Northern states. The Sun Belt is known for its warm climate, extended summers, and relatively short and mild winters. The number of people drawn to the Sun Belt has grown dramatically since the 1960s largely because of the migration of baby-boomers to this area and increased economic opportunities for business growth.

**Superego.** In Freudian theory, the id, ego, and superego are the three parts of psyche. According to Freud, the id is the impulsive component that urges actors to act. The ego is the realistic part of the psyche that mediates between the impulses of the id and the restraints of the super-ego. The superego is the moralizing force of the psyche and so restrains the impulses of the id because those impulses conflict with social norms.

**Superordinate Goal.** A goal that can only be achieved by cooperation among people who share that same goal.

**Surplus Value.** According to Marx, surplus value is obtained at the expense of the workers—the "have-nots." Specifically, it is the difference between the value of the finished product to the consumer and the value of the materials and labor that went into the manufacture of the product.

**Survey Research.** A type of research method that utilizes structured survey, either in print or available on the Internet, to collect data. Survey research is the most common type of research utilized in sociology and can be either quantitative or qualitative in nature. Advantages of survey research include: (1) answers are easily quantifiable as data, (2) large groups can be studied, (3) researchers can employ others to collect response data, (4) survey research is quick, and (5) inexpensive when compared to other designs. Disadvantages of survey research include: (1) research findings might be superficial or doubtful, and (2) return rates may be low and therefore challenge the validity and reliability of the study.

**Symbols.** Any object or action that conveys meaning through a process of interpreting the symbol within the context it is occurring. Symbols define the situation. For instance, if we were attending a wedding and noticed a woman crying several rows in front of us, we would likely interpret her tears as "tears of joy." But after the wedding, as we across a park to our car, we notice a young woman sitting on a park bench crying. It is likely we would interpret her tears as an indication she was sad or depressed. So, even though the symbol we are interpreting is the same, tears, we interpret those tears differently because the context has changed.

**Symbolic Interaction Theory.** One of the major theoretical perspectives in sociology, and though Blumer coined the term in 1937, sociologist George Herbert Mead is credited as the founder of symbolic interactionism. The perspective argues that people interact with each other and social institutions on the basis of the consensual interpretation of shared symbols. These shared meanings allow for the social construction of reality. Only when people are in agreement as to the interpretations of these symbols is there meaning.

**Taboo.** Because taboo violations threaten the survival of the society, a violation of a taboo always carries severe sanctions (e.g., the death penalty or imprisonment). Examples of taboo violations would include incest, mass murder, and cannibalism. For instance, in 1972, a rugby team from a college in Uruguay was flying to a match in Peru when the plane they were on crashed into the Andes mountains. After about eight weeks of being stranded on the mountain, 16 survivors were rescued, but 29 had died by the time rescuers arrived. Within a few days of their rescue, survivors were forced to admit that they had survived by eating the flesh of those who had died. As Catholics, cannibalism was considered a mortal sin (i.e., a sin so grievous that those committing it would go to Hell). However, the Archbishop of Montevideo absolved survivors of their sin because the preservation of their lives was considered more important than the act of cannibalism.

**Tactful Blindness.** Used by Goffman to explain how individuals purposefully ignore mistakes or blunders in the interaction process; used to explain interaction rituals as in terms of theatrical performances.

**Taylor, Frederick.** Frederick Taylor (1856 – 1915) (right) is considered the father of scientific management and "Taylorism." Taylor is known for his time and motion studies. By adopting ideas from Adam Smith's works on breaking down work tasks for greater efficiency (found in Smith's book, *The Wealth of Nations*), Taylor believed, and then proved, how by adopting production methods to fit workers' abilities, productivity would be increased. See also, Scientific Management.

**Taylorism.** See Taylor, Frederick, and scientific management.

**Techniques of Neutralization.** Techniques or excuses made by adults and children who have been caught committing illegal activities. Those techniques include: (1) denying responsibility, (2) denying harm and injury, (3) blaming the victim, (4) denouncing authorities, and (5) invoking higher principles or authority. Techniques of neutralization allow perpetrators to maintain a relatively high self-image and even cast themselves in the role of victim.

**Technological Determinism.** The belief that social life in post-industrial societies is shaped by technological development.

**Technology.** Innovation that results from highly developed technical and scientific knowledge.

**Tension Release Theory.** As tensions increase between people in an exceedingly complex and interdependent social world, some sociologists believe that sport acts as something of a pressure safety-valve allowing people to vent their frustrations and anger in a relatively harmless manner. However, sport does not always allow people to vent those frustrations and anger harmlessly as the theory suggests. See also, Hooliganism.

**Terrorism.** Terrorism is the use of violence, or threat of violence, by a minority group to achieve its religious or political goals. It should be noted that defining groups as terrorists, or specific behaviors as terroristic acts, it is the dominant group or power that does so. Terrorism is designed to intimidate a people. Individuals, religions, and political states throughout history have used terrorism as a tactic. For instance, during the American Civil War, residents of Lawrence, Kansas (Kansas had previously voted to remain with the Union), were attacked by bands of pro-Confederate bands, most notably Quantrill's Raiders, and it is thought that hundreds of civilian men, women, and children were massacred. Likewise, during World War II, the Germans bombed the English city of Coventry killing approximately 1,200 civilians. In 1945, British and American bombers raided the German city of Dresden with incendiary bombs killing approximately 23,000 civilians. The Nazi government immediately called the attack an act of terrorism—though it did not classify its own attack on Coventry in the same way. Today, the deliberate attack on civilians is considered a war crime under the Geneva Convention. More recently, ISIS is probably the most widely-known terrorist group—brutally murdering men, women and children.

**Theoretical Approach.** Using theory, social or otherwise, as a guiding force in attempting to explain some phenomenon.

**Theory.** Theory, in general, is a statement of how and why facts are related. A theory attempts to explain why, how, or when things happen. Theories contain concepts, propositions, and are preceded by axioms. See also, social theory.

**Theory of Planned Behavior.** The link between attitudes and behavior is actually poor. People may say one thing but not do what they said they would do. The theory of planned behavior suggests that you can only predict that a person will follow through on their expressed intention to perform a certain action when three things are known: their attitude toward the behavior itself, subjective norms, and their belief that the behavior will pay off for them. For instance, studying. A student might say they plan on studying for an exam, but may not end up doing so. However, if the student believes that studying is a good thing, that his or her friends believe in the efficacy of studying, and that by studying they will most likely earn a good grade, it is likely they will study.

**Theory X.** Developed by Douglas McGregor, Theory X is a style of management, which suggests that workers need to be strictly supervised and punished for activities that restrict production. The theory views workers as hating their jobs, avoiding responsibility, resist change, and do not care about the needs of the organization. This management style is authoritarian in nature.

**Theory Y.** In this theory of organizational management, McGregor suggests that workers should be motivated to be productive, responsible, and engaged in the betterment of the organization by increasing their job satisfaction—both intrinsically and extrinsically.

**Theory Z.** Building on Douglas McGregor's work, William Ouchi, believed that by providing life-long employment to workers and providing for their well-being, the loyalty of workers would increase and with it productivity, high morale, and overall job satisfaction.

**Thomas Theorem.** See below.

**Thomas, W.I.** In the 1920s, W. I. Thomas developed the idea of that situations were defined by social actors (i.e., the definition of the situation). Perhaps the most widely accepted sociological and social psychological notion could be found in Thomas' words, "If men define situations as real, they are real in their consequences." It is similar in meaning to another widely accepted belief in sociology, the social construction of reality. In other words, man in his social world, and through the use of consensual interpretation of symbols, constructs reality.

**Total Institution.** Places where individuals are isolated from the rest of society and their activities are tightly controlled and regulated. For example, North Korea.

**Totalitarianism.** A form of autocracy and authoritarianism that involves the use of state power to control and regulate all phases of life. The three characteristics of the totalitarian state are: (1) the state has unlimited power, (2) the state tolerates no opposition, and (3) the state exercises close control over its citizens. Examples include Hitler, Stalin, Saddam Hussein.

**Tracking.** Tracking is the practice of putting students on specific paths based on their scholastic ability, curriculum, or gender.

**Traditional Authority.** Authority that is passed down over time and generations. For instance, in the U.S. some believe that political parties have traditional authority because their existence goes back substantially in time and they hold significant power and authority.

**Transformational Leader.** A style of leadership where subordinates work with a leader to identify a problem, develop a plan to address the problem, and then work as a team to implement that solution.

**Transsexuals.** People who feel they are one sex, though biologically they are the other.

**Triad.** A group consisting of three individuals engaged in social interaction.

# U

**Underclass.** In a highly stratified system, the lowest of the low--the poorest and most disadvantaged in society.

**Underemployment.** The hiring of employees that have more experience or education than is required for the job. These employees almost always earn significantly less than what their training and education is worth in the labor force, but a downturn in the economy forces them to take jobs that do not value their training or education. Also, many employers will not hire candidates who are over-qualified because they fear the employee will move on to a higher paying job after the hiring organization has incurred a financial cost to training them for their specific job.

**Underground Economy.** Exchanges of goods and services that occur outside of the normal economy. The "black market" is an example of the underground economy.

**Unfocused Interaction.** Unfocused interactions are when there is mutual awareness that people have of one another in large gatherings even though they may not directly be involved in conversation. For instance, let's say you walk into a party, there are many people at the party and most are talking to other people. The room is filled with conversation, but you are not directly involved in any of those conversations-you simply know that they are occurring. That would be an example of an unfocused interaction.

**Unintended Symbols.** Also known as expressions given-off. Those symbols that we'd rather others didn't see and interpret. For instance, sweating during a job interview or having a quivering voice during that same job interview.

**Unit of Analysis.** Who or what is being studied in a piece of social research.

**Unsocialized Children.** Severe social isolation contributes to poor social development. Depending on the severity and duration of the isolation, long-term consequences can be severe and even lead to death. For example, in 1970 an elderly woman walked into a social services agency with a 13-year old girl in tow. The girl was emaciated, pale, walked in a strange manner, and was unable to speak. Workers got suspicious and began asking questions. What they found out astonished them. They named the girl "Genie" in order to keep her real identity confidential. At the age of four, Genie's father was so convinced she was mentally retarded that he confined her to her room. During the day, she was chained to a potty-chair, and at night she was put into a crib with a chicken wire top that kept her from climbing out. Genie remained in that state of isolation for nine years—from the age of four until the age of thirteen. Social workers began working with her intensely to repair the emotional and intellectual damage done by the years of isolation. At first, they were successful and Genie learned a few words she could speak and her walking greatly improved. However, after several years Genie stopped learning and in fact regressed to an earlier stage. As of this writing, Genie is still alive (above) and has spent her time since being rescued living in a nursing home as she is incapable of living independently.

In another more recent case, a man grew suspicious and called the police because he had not seen his neighbor's young daughter for several years. When the police investigated, they found that the girl, who was age six at the time, had been confined to her bedroom since the age of two. The girl used the corner of her bedroom as a latrine. Conditions were appalling. Once removed from the home, counselors began working with the girl in an effort to repair the emotional and intellectual damage that had been done. Unlike with Genie, results were much better. Psychologists believe the reason they were successful in the latter, but not in Genie's case, is because of the age difference. Significant brain changes occur in children around the age of 10, and it changes the way we learn.

Other studies have found even more alarming negative effects of social isolation. In a 1945 study involving human babies, Spitz followed the social development of babies who were removed from their mothers early in life. Some children were placed with foster families while others were raised in nursing homes. The nursing home babies had no family-like environment as the setting was very institutional. Care was provided by nurses who worked eight-hour shifts. More than a third of those raised in the nursing homes died and 21 were still living in nursing or mental institutions after 40 years. The isolation resulted in their lifelong physical, mental, or social retardation.

**Upper Class.** In a class system, those at the top with the greatest amount of resources--wealth, power, and privilege.

**Urbanization** The growth of cities.

**Utilitarian Organization.** Formal organization that people join with a specific goal in mind. Sociologists point out that most people join this type of organization with a remunerative goal in mind.

**Validity (research).** This is the degree to which a measure (e.g., an index or scale) really reflects what is being studied. It is largely associated with the process of operationalizing variables.

**Value-Added Theory.** A theory suggesting that many instances of collective behavior represent efforts to change the social environment.

**Values.** Shared, stated but often abstract, ideals that people of a given culture consider important. For instance, as Americans we value the ideal of equality, but in practice, not all Americans share the same interpretation of equality (e.g., prejudice and discrimination).

**Variable.** Any factor, trait, or condition that can exist in differing amounts or types. Generally, there are three types of variables: (1) independent, which is manipulated, (2) dependent, which means the variable is dependent on how the independent variable is manipulated, and (3) a controlled variable, which is held constant and usually only used in experiments which occur in highly controlled situations. An example of an independent variable would be age, while an example of a dependent variable might be income (which would be dependent on the independent variable of number of years of education).

**Veblen, Thorstein.** Thorstein Bunde Veblen (1857 – 1929) was an American economist and sociologist and known for his profound criticism of capitalism. He is most notably known for development of his concept conspicuous consumption. Veblen believed that the massive consumption of goods and services socially demonstrated the higher social status of the wealthy.

**Verbal Communication.** Social interaction involves nonverbal communication as well as verbal communication. Verbal communication requires both language and para-language, whereas nonverbal communication involves such things as body language, eye contact, and facial expression.

**Verstehen.** Max Weber's belief that actors can understand each other's motives and behaviors.

**Vertical Mobility.** Movement of an individual up, down or laterally on a hierarchy of status. See also, intragenerational mobility and intergenerational mobility.

**Victimless Crime.** Crimes like prostitution and gambling where laws are broken but there are no identifiable "victims."

**Wallerstein, Immanuel.** Immanuel Maurice Wallerstein (1930 – present) is an American sociologist best known for his work on world-systems theory. World systems theory proposes that there is a world economic system that benefited some countries but exploited others. Wallerstein credits theorists like Marx for his social views and McCarthyism for his political views. (McCarthyism is when primarily politicians make accusations of subversion without proof or even little in the way of evidence).

**War.** Often the result of failed political resolutions to a dispute between nations, war is the resulting armed conflict.

**Wealth.** The total financial value of what a person possesses in the way of income and assets.

**Weber, Max.** Max Weber (1864-1920) was a German sociologist known for his work on bureaucratic organizations. Weber proposed that there were three components that all bureaucracies should adopt: (1) rationality—the ability to use reason and observable facts to explain events, (2) impersonality—that treatment should be based on equality, and (3) meritocracy—that jobs in these organizations should be filled by people who held skills and expertise relevant to that position.

**Weberian Approach** The views held by conflict theorists who, using the ideas of Max Weber, stress the significance of conflict in social life, especially conflict among status groups such as those based on occupation, ethnic background, or religion.

**Welfare.** A term often misused by the general public to refer to people, primarily African-American women, receiving money from the government undeservedly. In fact, the term refers to a specific program called Aid to Families with Dependent Children. In absolute numbers, there more Caucasian women receiving AFDC than Black women, the vast majority of women who receive AFDC work full-time jobs.

**Welfare Capitalism.** A market-based economy that offers social welfare programs to its citizenry like free health care and education to the masses.

**Welfare Dependency.** Dependence on various state-sponsored programs.

**White Collar.** Generally, refers to middle class workers in a class system.

**White-Collar Crime.** Crimes committed by people in a position of authority and high social status within an organization. Because they are trusted, and have a great deal of autonomy, it is much harder to expose white-collar crime than other types of crime. Edwin Sutherland (1883 – 1950) was the first to coin the term "white collar crime" at an American Sociological Association conference in a 1939 speech. White-collar crimes include fraud, bankruptcy fraud, bribery, insider trading, embezzlement, computer crime, medical crime, public corruption, identity theft, environmental crime, pension fund crime, RICO (i.e., Racketeer Influenced and Corrupt Organizations Act) crimes, consumer fraud, occupational crime, securities fraud, financial fraud, and forgery.

**Working Class.** Generally, lower class workers who have some skills and sell their labor to the higher classes. Also known as blue collar workers.

**Working Poor.** Generally, workers with few job skills, are seen as easily replaceable, and often have cyclical patterns of leaving and entering the paid labor force due to lay-offs and periods of unemployment.

**World System Theory.** As societies industrialize, Wallerstein predicted that capitalism would become the dominant economic system and this would eventually lead to the globalization of capitalism as the only economic system.

**Xenophobia.** Fear of foreigners or immigrants.

# Part II: Study Questions

# Section 1: Questions on Sociological Approach

## 1.1 What is Sociology?

Sociology is the study of society and human behavior.

## 1.2 What is special about the way sociologists approach topics?

The subject matter of sociology is quite often invisible or not directly observable. However, sociologists can observe the consequences of such social characteristics as group pressure, authority, prestige and culture. They then form images of these concepts using what C. Wright Mills has called the sociological imagination taking into account the influence in order to view their own society as an outsider might.

## 1.3 What sort of questions do sociologists address?

Sociologists want to understand:
(a) what goes on in and between groups of people;
(b) what are the social differences we observe;
(c) what is happening in social institutions;
(d) why and how social change is occurring.

## 1.4 What are theories, concepts and propositions and how are they used?

A sociological issue is a question we seek to answer with a theory or general explanation of a social phenomenon. A concept is a category of behavior, events or characteristics that are considered similar for the sake of theory construction. A proposition is a statement that explains one concept by means of another. If we seek to discover why racial groups sometimes live in harmony and sometimes do not, we may use the concept of racial harmony to describe the differing ways of relating. The behavior is defined as indicating harmony exists. We would then state our theory in propositions. For example, different racial groups will live in harmony in situations where enough work exists for all groups to earn a decent living.

## 1.5 How did the discipline of sociology develop?

Sociology developed in the midst of the social and intellectual upheaval surrounding the Industrial Revolution of the 19th century. Three branches of sociology grew from roots in three interest groups:
1. social activists,
2. a new breed of scientists dedicated to applying the scientific approach

    to society,
3. and philosophers interested in humanity's social nature.

**1.6 What is the place of Marx, Comte, Spencer, Durkheim, Mead and Weber in the development of sociology?**
- Karl Marx was the first major proponent of the conflict perspective. He believed that inequality between classes causes conflict between groups of people and that society must change in order to fulfil the needs of all the people.
- Auguste Comte was the French scientist who gave sociology its name and promoted the scientific study of society.
- Herbert Spencer extended Comte's work developing the idea that society was an organic whole that could be studied much like the human body. This was the beginnings of structural-functionalism.
- In Émile Durkheim's classic study on anomie and suicide rates, he also promoted sociology as a science and structural functionalism as a perspective with his emphasis on social facts explaining other social facts.
- George Herbert Mead focused on how we use symbols, including language and how our use of symbols influences our social development and social life.
- Max Weber's analysis of the major dynamics of society and social change provides the foundations for much of the sociological theory and research of our time. His study "The Protestant Ethic and the Spirit of Capitalism" was an important study of the roots of the industrial revolution, which was sweeping the world in his day.

**1.7 What are the basic concepts of structural-functionalism, the conflict approach and symbolic-interactionism?**

Structural-functionalism assumes that order is dominant in society and that social arrangements arise and persist because they serve society and its members well. The conflict approach assumes the dominant process in society is conflict and that society divides into two groups the masses and small elite who exploit them. The symbolic-interaction perspective assumes that the important action in society takes place around the use of symbols that channel our thoughts and thereby define what is socially comprehensible and incomprehensible. Practitioners of this approach often focus on interaction among individuals in contrast to the other perspective which tend to look more at social institutions.

**1.8 What are the contributions of Mills, Collins, Parsons, Davis, Thomas and Goffman to the development of these theories?**
- C. Wright Mills effectively promoted a general conflict perspective in

the U.S. focusing on social class differences and introducing the concept of power elite; a tiny minority of government, military and business figures believed to control the U.S.
- Randal Collins is one of the most articulate voices today from that perspective and he developed a formal theory of conflict applicable to all levels of society; especially analyzing the inequalities in the American educational system.
- Talcott Parsons extended Durkheim's tradition into the 20th century developing the idea that society could be viewed as a system that must adapt to changes in its environment, pursue its goals, integrate itself with other systems and maintain order within itself much like a biological organism.
- Kingsley Davis is a major contemporary proponent of this structural-functionalism perspective and he analyses wealth and poverty from this viewpoint.
- W. I. Thomas extended Mead's ideas, theorizing that people define or construct their own social reality and that their definitions become real because they are real in their consequences.
- Erving Goffman has served as a major contemporary spokesperson for the symbolic interaction perspective and he describes how people present themselves in everyday life in order to manage the impression they give to others.

## 1.9 What is the scientific method and how can it be applied to the study of sociology?

The scientific method involves eight basic steps:
1. Observation of an event that stimulates thinking.
2. Defining or classifying the terms or events being considered.
3. Formulating the research issue or hypothesis.
4. Generating a theory or proposition - a general statement that serves as a potential answer to the research question.
5. Creating a research design in order to test whether the theory or proposition is valid.
6. Collecting data-working through the research design to make observations.
7. Analyzing the data.
8. Making conclusions and evaluating the theory.

## 1.10 What are the advantages and disadvantages of the survey method, analysis of existing sources, observational study and experimental research in the study of sociology?

A survey is a research method in which a representative sample of a population is asked to respond to questions. In principle, every member of the population has an equal chance of being selected so the survey should give an accurate representation of the views of a population. However, people may try to answer questions as they think the survey interviewer wants them to thus biasing the results of the research.

Analysis of existing sources is a research technique in which the researcher uses existing documents that were created for some other purpose. This research generally costs much less than the survey allows access to otherwise unavailable subjects and to date over long periods of time and involves data that is not influenced by the interviewer. Documents used however may be biased toward their original purpose and thus distort the true picture the researcher is trying to find.

In an observational study the researcher actually witness social behavior in its natural setting either as a participant or an unobtrusive observer. The advantage of this study is that research is accomplished by directly observing subjects' behavior thus permitting access to nonverbal as well as verbal behavior. Observation also allows for study over a time rather than at one point.

An experiment is a research design in which the researcher exposes a group of subjects to a treatment and observes its effect usually in comparison to a similar control group that did not receive the treatment. Experiments can demonstrate clearly that a variable has a particular effect on the subject group because the researcher retains maximum control over the circumstances of the research. Experiments are very expensive. Sometimes an aspect of the experiment other than the treatment is the real cause of the experiment's outcome but this goes unnoticed and the artificiality of many experimental settings makes generalizing to natural settings risky.

**1.11 What are some of the challenges and ethical issues in the study of sociology?**

Sociology faces the challenge of working with human beings and their social groupings because people have rights that limit what we can do with them while we are studying them. Sociological subjects can give us important information but their information can be distorted. Sociologists must decide whether their own views will influence their research and theory development. By believing that knowledge is neutral or that value neutrality is either naïve or a rationalization for the fact that one is working for the elite because most sociological research is funded by and disproportionately available to powerful elites.

## Section 2: Questions on Society

**How do subsistence adaptation and technology help in the process of sorting societies?**

We can identify six types of societies by focusing on the dominant form of work in a society or subsistence adaptation. In hunting and gathering societies, people live by hunting wild animals using primitive weapons and gathering food as it grows naturally. Herding or pastoral, societies often arise in areas with poor soil and rely on the domestication of animals into herds as a major means of support, linked with either hunting and gathering or other technology. The semi-permanent horticulture produces its food through cultivation of the soil with hand tools and is more common in areas with fertile soil, which is exhausted within three to five years. Agricultural societies employ animal-drawn plows to cultivate the land and often combine this with irrigation to increase productivity. In industrial societies, the largest portion of the labor force is involved in mechanized production of goods and services.

**What are the elements of social structure?**

Social structure is the enduring patterns of social behavior including statuses, roles, norms and institutions that constitute relatively stable relations in society. A status is a position in a particular social pattern. A role includes the behavior that goes with but is distinct from the status.

**What are two ways in which status is conferred?**

Status is either conferred independently of the individual's efforts or abilities (ascribed) or attained through effort or performance (achieved).

**What is a status intervention, and how might it affect a group?**

A status intervention is an attempt to diminish the influence of an undesirable status characteristic. Research shows that groups will discount the input of persons with low status characteristics and be overly positive toward the input of persons with high status characteristics even if the status has nothing to do with the task of the group at the time. People of low status can be taught to be assertive in their own realm by learning that people of higher status do not necessarily know more about everything.

**What are postindustrial societies and how are they distinguished from industrial societies?**

In a post-industrial society, increasingly sophisticated virtually automatic machines take over much unskilled work and the majority of the labor force becomes employed in service occupations. Government becomes more involved in realms that were previously dominated by the other institutions of society: family, religion, education and the economy. This form of society might be thought of as a service society or an information based society.

**What are the major differences between modern and pre-modern societies?**

According to Durkheim, pre-modern societies are held together by mechanical solidarity or bonds of common activities and values as opposed to modern societies that are held together by organic solidarity or bonds based on interdependence. Ferdinand Tonnies used the labels Gemeinschalf, or community, and Gesellschalf, or simple associations centered around task completion to describe similar differences. Modern societies have more complexity in occupational structure, more formal relationships, and more reliance on nonfamily institutions and less reliance on custom to regulate behavior.

**What is the essential nature of the basic social processes?**
- Conflict is the process in which the parties struggle against one another for a commonly prized object - for example wars and feuds.
- Coercion is a process of being forced to act against one's will, as in slavery.
- Exploitation, a process in which one is deprived of things that one rightfully is due. For example, when illegal migrant workers are underpaid they have no means of recourse.
- Competition involves two or more parties seeking a goal that is not available to them all- for instance getting a contract to build a bank.
- Cooperation is a social process in which the parties involved act jointly to bring about mutual benefit, either as a result of traditional values, direction of an authority figure or a contract.

**How do conflict and functionalist theories view social processes?**

Structural-functionalists assume that cooperation is part of the nature of society and they look for ways in which the structure functions to maintain society. Conflict theorists assume that conflict is intrinsic to society and examine society for signs of conflict, coercion and exploitation.

# Section 3: Questions on Doing Sociological Research

**What is sociological research?**

Sociological research is used by sociologists to answer questions and in many cases test hypotheses. The research method someone uses depends on the question that is asked.

**Is sociological research scientific?**

Sociological research is derived from the scientific method, meaning that it relies on empirical observation and, sometimes the testing of hypotheses.

**What is the difference between qualitative research and quantitative research?**

Qualitative research is relatively unstructured, does not rely heavily upon statistics, and is closely focused on a question being asked. Quantitative research uses statistical methods. Both kinds of research are used in sociology.

**What are some of the statistical concepts in sociology?**

Through research, sociologists are able to make statements of probability, or likelihood. Sociologists use percentages and rates. The mean is the same as an average. The median represents the midpoint in an array of values or scores. The mode is the most common value or score. Correlation and cross-tabulation are statistical procedures that allow sociologists to see how two (or more) different variables are associated.

**What different tools of research do sociologists use?**
The most common tools of sociological research are surveys and interviews, participant observation, controlled experiments, content analysis, comparative and historical research, and evaluation research. Each method has its own strengths and weaknesses. You can better generalize from surveys than participant observation, but participant observation is better for capturing subtle nuances and depth in social behavior.

## Section 4: Questions on Culture

### How do sociologists define culture?

Culture is the values, norms, language, tools and other shared products of society that provide a plan for social life.

### What do functionalists see as the functions of culture?

Functionalists suggest that culture provides for continuing social order by handing down prescribed ways of behaving in specific situations and allows people to benefit from the achievements of previous generations.

### What are norms and why are they important?

Norms are shared rules or guidelines for behavior in specific situations. The strongest norms are taboos or rules that prohibit certain behavior and carry severe punishment for violators. Norms carry sanctions or rewards for behavior that conform to a norm and punishment for behavior that violates a norm. Institutions are organized sets of norms, values, statuses and roles that are centered on the basic needs of society. The five basic institutions of most societies are: the family, religion, the state, the economic system and education.

### How do values underlie norms?

Values are shared ideas about what is right and wrong, good and bad, desirable and undesirable. Values are the general concepts on which our specific norms are built.

### How do norms vary between cultures?

Many norms are specific to one society or to one group in a society for example most college students in the United States share a norm against turning in a fellow student for cheating.

### What are the symbolic elements of culture?

A symbol is that which represents something else. Norms and values are often transmitted within a culture or to other cultures through symbolic elements such as language, gesture and stance, style of clothing, hairstyle, social distance, time, and use of symbolic representation such as flags.

**What is the importance of language in transmitting culture?**
Most social scientists see a strong connection between a society's language and the rest of its culture. Language reflects what is important to that society to its new members and those outside of the culture. Our silent language or nonverbal space and time messages are also tied to our culture.

**How do cultures vary?**

Cultures differ in their degree of complexity. They can be focused around kinship or institutions and the pace of change. In simple societies kinship organizes people's lives around families. Such societies might change rather slowly compared to modern postindustrial society.

**How do the functional, ecological, evolutionary, conflict and symbolic interactionist approaches explain cultural variation?**

- The functional approach suggests that a functional cultural trait has a positive consequence for the society and will probably not be adopted unless it fits well with the existing culture and contributes to the well-being of the society.
- The ecological approach shows how societies adapt culture to their physical environment in order to survive thus making it a subform of the functional approach.
- The evolutionary approach views culture as developing through a series of stages toward forms that are increasingly well suited to the environment based on changes in the culture's basic tools or technology.
- The conflict approach points out that prevailing definition of beauty, justice and truth may serve the elites at the expense of the masses with culture being created and imposed on the masses by the ruling class.
- The symbolic interactionist approach highlights the importance of symbols in understanding culture and the social behavior it shapes, suggesting that symbols are the major agent for transmitting and shaping culture.

**How do subcultures and countercultures differ from the dominant culture?**

A subculture is the culture of a subgroup of society that adopts norms that set them apart from the dominant group. For instance, persons who live in a Chinatown but are integrated into the life of the city as a whole. A counterculture is a subculture whose norms and values are not just different from but in conflict with those of the dominant culture.

**How do cultural universalism and cultural relativism differ?**
Some sociologists believe that cultural universals or traits are common to all human societies. Others suggest that each culture should be studied only in relation to itself and not be judged by external cultural standards or by a universal standard a stance known as cultural relativism.

**How does ethnocentrism affect one's viewpoint?**

Ethnocentrism is the tendency to use one's own cultural values in evaluating the beliefs and customs of other cultures with different values. It can be useful to a society in that it bonds members together, but can also lead to conflict with people from other cultures.

# Section 5: Questions on Socialization

### How does socialization shape a person's self-image?

To some extent, we accept the definitions of ourselves that we are taught by our families and other members of our society.

### What does Cooley mean by looking glass self?

Cooley decided that a person comes to think of himself or herself as an "I" through a combination of biological and social processes. The looking glass self is the image of self that a person sees reflected by others.

### How does Mead explain people taking the role of the other?

Mead believes people take the role of the other by progressing through three stages. In stage I the infant is all "I". The "me" begins to develop through play in stage II and fully develops as the child learns to respond to the generalized other in stage III, taking into account the broader social community. Significant others or persons with whom an individual has intimate and long-term contact facilitate this process. This self-awareness makes it possible for people to position themselves within larger social units.

### What is Goffman's contribution to the idea of the social self?

Goffman points out that the socialization process continues into adulthood. He discusses for instance, impression management, or how in daily activity we alter ourselves to fit the audience we are addressing, a process made up of thousands of small everyday social responses.

### What is sociobiology and why is it controversial?

Sociobiology introduced by Edward Wilson is the systematic study of the biological basis of social behavior in every kind of organism. Wilson believes that human social behavior rests on a genetic foundation. His ideas have created controversy because they could conceivably be used to promote racist and sexist policies.

### What are three modes of socialization?

Socialization occurs through explicit instruction, conditioning, and innovation and role modeling. In practice, these modes are usually blended.

### What are three characteristics of the socialization process?
The socialization process tends to be general rather than specific, calls forth automatic behaviors and responses and persists through time.

### What are the basic agents of socialization or domination?

The family, peer groups, television, daycare and schools are today's basic agents of socialization. Conflict theorists point out that these agents can be thought of as agents of domination because they may use their position to perpetuate an unequal power situation and to dominate the one being socialized.

### What are the basic thesis of Erikson, Piaget, Kohlberg and Gilligan?
- Erikson presented an eight-stage theory of personality development in which each stage may be positively resolved or unresolved. He stressed that the close interaction between the social environment and personality.
- Piaget suggests that everyone passes through four major intellectual stages: Sensory-motor, preoperational, concrete operations and formal operations. He believes that social contact is necessary for advancing through the stages.
- Kohlberg: Moral decisions based on fear of punishment, idea of rewards taken into account, immediate punishments and rewards not necessary, strict adherence to rules, recognition that conventional rules may come into conflict with a higher sense of right and wrong and universal principles of justice, human rights and human dignity guide decisions.
- Gilligan: When women reach the upper stages of moral development their decisions are guided by the principle of protecting relationships and people rather than by the principle of individual rights that guides men's decisions.

### How does socialization continue in adulthood?

Socialization in adulthood is more concerned with learning overt norms and behaviors than is the socialization of childhood, which is concerned primarily with regulating antisocial behavior. Levinson's work suggests that successfully completing the transitions between our life stages is of crucial importance in leading a fulfilling life. Resocialization may occur in adulthood when an individual commits himself or herself to a new goal or enters a total institution.

### In what ways is socialization important to society as a whole?

Society as a whole may encourage or discourage the development of individual characteristics. A genius can grow in a social group more easily if the intellectual atmosphere of the group nurtures genius. Nisbet urges that we protect our social setting to provide experiences that foster the growth of genius in our society.

# Section 6: Questions on Social Interaction

### What is Society?

Society is a system of social interaction that includes both culture and social organization. Society includes social institutions, or established organized social behavior, and exists for a recognized purpose. Social structure is the patterned relationships within a society. Two other forms of social organization also contribute to the cohesion of a society: Gemeinschaft, a "community" characterized by cohesion based on friendships and loyalties, and Gesellschaft, a "society," characterized by cohesion based on complexity and differentiation and task completion.

### What are the Types of Societies?

Societies across the globe vary in type, as determined mainly by the complexity of their social structures, their division of labor, and their technologies. From least to most complex, they are hunting and gathering, pastoral, agricultural, industrial, and postindustrial societies.

### What are the Forms of Social Interaction in Society?

All forms of social interaction in society are shaped by the structure of its social institutions. A group is a collection of individuals who interact and communicate with each other, share goals and norms, and have a subjective awareness of themselves as a distinct social unit. Status is a hierarchical position in a structure; a role is the expected behavior associated with a particular status. A role is the behavior others expect from a person associated with a particular status.

### What Theories are there about Social Interaction?

Social interaction takes place in society within the context of social structure and social institutions. Social interaction is analyzed in several ways, including the social construction of reality where we impose meaning and reality on our interactions with others; ethnomethodology which is deliberate interruption of interaction to observe how a return to normal interaction is accomplished; impression management allows a person to manage the impression of themselves using face-work while they are "on stage."

### How is Technology changing Social Interaction?

Increasingly, people engage with each other through cyberspace interaction. Social norms develop in cyberspace as they do in face-to-face interaction, but a person in cyberspace can also manipulate their impression easily, and with a greater chance of deception, that they can do when meeting face-to-face.

# Section 7: Questions on Social Organization, Groups, and Bureaucracies

### What are the types of groups?

Groups are a fact of human existence and permeate virtually every facet of our lives. Group size is important, as is the otherwise simple distinction between dyads and triads. Primary groups (i.e., family and close friends) form the basic building blocks of social interaction in society. Reference groups play a major role in forming our attitudes and life goals, as do our relationships with in-groups and out-groups. Social networks partly determine things such as whom we know and the kinds of jobs we get. Networks based on race-ethnicity, social class, and other social factors are extremely closely connected very dense.

### How strong is social influence?

The social influence groups exert on us is tremendous, as seen by the Asch conformity experiments. Milgram's experiments demonstrated that the interpersonal influence of an authority figure could cause an individual to act against his or her deep convictions. The torture and abuse of Iraqi prisoners of war by American soldiers as prison guards serves as testimony to the powerful effects of both social influence and authority structures.

### What is the importance of groupthink and risky shift?

Groupthink can be so pervasive that it adversely affects group decision-making. Risky shift similarly often compels individuals to reach decisions that are at odds with their better judgement.

### What are the types of formal organizations and bureaucracies, and what are some of their problems?

There are several types of formal organizations, such as normative, coercive, or utilitarian. Weber typified bureaucracies as organizations with an efficient division of labor, an authority hierarchy, rules, impersonal relationships, and career ladders. Bureaucratic rigidities often result in organizational problems such as ritualism and resulting "normalization of deviance", which may have been significantly responsible for the space shuttle Challenger explosion in 1986 and the space shuttle Columbia breakup in 2003. The McDonaldization of society has resulted in greater efficiency, calculability, and control in many industries, probably at the expense of some individual creativity.

### What are the problems of diversity in organizations?

Formal organizations perpetuate society's inequalities on the basis of race-ethnicity, gender, and social class. Even today, Blacks, Hispanics, and Native Americans are less likely to get promoted, and more likely to get fired, than Whites of comparable education and other qualifications. Women experience similar effects of inequality, especially negative effects of tokenism, such as stress and lowered self-esteem. Finally, persons of less than middle-class origins make less money and are less likely to get promoted than a middle-class person of comparable education.

**What do the functional, conflict and symbolic interaction theories say about organizations?**

Functional, conflict, and symbolic interaction theories highlight and clarify the analysis of organizations by specifying both organizational functions and dysfunctions (functional theory); by analyzing the consequences of hierarchical, gender, race, and social class conflict in organizations (conflict theory); and, finally, by studying the importance of social interaction and integration of the self into the organization (symbolic interaction theory).

**What is a group?**

A group is a set of people recurrently interacting in a structured way according to shared expectations about each other's behavior.

**What is the difference between primary and secondary groups?**

A primary group is based on intimate, face-to-face interaction whereas a secondary group is less cohesive, more formal and less supportive of members.

**How important is social support to the quality and length of life?**

Social support has been found to significantly increase an individual's satisfaction with life, promote health and well-being of individuals and reduce the effects of stress in a person's life. People who have supportive primary group relationships also live longer.

**How do small groups differ in structure, leadership, size and membership?**

A small group is a collection of people who meet more or less regularly in face to face interaction who possess a common identity or exclusiveness of purpose and who share a set of standards governing their activities. Their structure can be formal - public and explicit or informal private and implicit depending on the needs of the group members. The nature of a group's structure often depends on its central person. As groups grow, they are likely to develop formal structures that are increasingly elaborate. Even numbered groups are more characterized by disagreement and conflict than odd numbered groups.

### How do leaders emerge within groups?

Members who have the highest rate of group participation are most often chosen to be leaders. Other traits associated with leadership are intelligence, enthusiasm, dominance, self-confidence and egalitarianism. Democratic leadership is most useful when there is sufficient time to involve the entire group in decisions.

### How do groups influence individual perception and behavior?

Groups generally reward members who conform to their norms. Group opinion strongly influences individual behavior and judgement toward that of the group. Homan's exchange theory states that people try to maximize rewards and minimize costs in social transactions and will conform to the group under these conditions. Deindividuation occurs when a person feels submerged in a large group that has strong feelings of group unity and focuses on external goals. The lack of self-awareness that results may cause pressure toward group conformity.

### How is group decision- making different from individual decision-making?

Group decision-making is much slower than individual, but group decisions tend to be more accurate. People in a group are sometimes willing to make decisions involving greater risk than they would alone. Groups first orient themselves, evaluate control over the expression of negative and positive reactions and then achieve solidarity in making a decision. In some cases, groups seek concurrence so strongly that groupthink occurs, creating a situation in which alternatives are not viewed realistically but only in terms of making the group members happy with each other. This can be combated by the leader being receptive to the opinions of everyone by asking for outside advice on the issue and by assigning group members to troubleshoot suggested options.

### What is a formal organization?

A formal organization is a group deliberately constructed to achieve specific objectives through explicitly defined roles and specified rules. Modern societies are characterized by the growth of such organizations and the reduction of primary groups.

### What are the stages in the development of bureaucracy?

Three conditions are necessary for the rise of bureaucracy: a money economy, a steady income to the bureaucracy and a large population base.

### What are the six characteristics of Weber's ideal bureaucracy?

Bureaucracies are large-scale, formal organizations that are highly differentiated and organized through elaborate policies and procedures in a hierarchy of authority. They are characterized by fixed division of labor, hierarchy of offices, written documents, management by trained experts, official work as the primary activity and management by rules.

### What are the functions and dysfunctions of modern bureaucracy?

Bureaucracy allows a society to accomplish large and complicated tasks, provides an efficient means for repetitive tasks and creates order in society. It also facilitates large-scale conflict by sometimes creating inappropriate or harmful rules, slowing upward communication of bad news, promoting antagonism between superiors and subordinates, perpetuating itself after it has served its purpose, growing beyond a size that is efficient, creating a situation in which workers feel dehumanized, creating a gulf between those at the top and those at the bottom and becoming a tool for exploitation. Robert Merton suggests that working in a bureaucracy for extended periods tends to entangle workers in rules, reinforcing timid and rigid attitudes among them.

### How does the Peter Principle work?

Peter Principle states that in a hierarchy competent employees tend to be promoted until they reach a level at which they are not competent to do the work, and then they remain there because they feel insecure about their shoddy work. They begin to concentrate on rules and regulations, reducing the quality of their work even more.

# Section 8: Questions on Deviance

**What do sociologists mean by social control and when do social controls influence behavior?**

Social control is the means by which members of a society attempt to induce each other to comply with the society's norms. Social controls influence behavior constantly because they are internalized and come into play every time a person has a deviant impulse.

**How do the various theories explain deviance?**

Social control theory argues that deviance is largely a matter of failed social controls. Merton believes that the strain between the norms that define socially appropriate goals and the norms that specify socially appropriate means for attaining these goals creates an atmosphere in which deviance will appear. Travis Hirschi says that persons with a weakened bond to their social group are likely to become deviant.

Differential association and cultural transmission theories propose that deviance is a natural outgrowth of a person's contacts during socialization and can be a part of a subculture that can be transmitted indefinitely.

Conflict theory traces the origin of criminal behavior to class conflict between the powerful and the weak and sees criminals as reasonable individuals forced by circumstance to break laws in order to regain some of what has been taken from them or denied to them by an exploitative system.

Functionalist theory proposes that deviance enhances feelings of unity within a society and helps define and redefine the norms. Labeling theory concentrates on the reactions of others to deviance and studies, which offenders are likely to be punished rather than which are likely to commit deviant acts.

Deterrence theory suggests that deviance increases as the perceived risk of being punished decreases and that people are more likely to be deviant if they think of themselves as deviant.

**How might anomie create a climate for deviance?**

Durkheim believed that an absence of clear norms for a society or an individual might create a social setting in which deviance will occur.

**What is the difference between deviance and deviants?**

Deviance is behavior that violates the norms of the social group in which the behavior occurs where as a deviant is one who is characterized as a violator of a norm. Engaging in deviant behavior does not automatically lead to a deviant reputation or self-image.

**How the mentally ill are treated?**

The mentally ill not only are treated as deviants but are feared. The fact that society treats them in this way increases their chances of being deviant in the future. The labeling of the mentally ill decreases their chances of future employment and of normal social relationships.

**How does society define crime?**

Crime is behavior that violates criminal law. It can be defined through laws, through official police reports of crime, or through victimization surveys of persons who have been involved in crime but perhaps not involved with the police department.

**Who are the criminals and how are they treated by society?**

A criminal is someone who has become publicly associated with the commission of a crime.

**What distinguishes white-collar crime and how might it be deterred?**

White-collar crime is crime committed by a person of responsibility and high social status in the course of his or her occupation. It differs from conventional crime in that the victims may be unaware of the crime and the offender may not view himself as a criminal. Deterrence of white-collar crime by regulatory agencies and internalized controls in organizations appears to be most promising.

## Section 9: Questions on Crime

### What is the difference between deviance and crime?

Deviance is behavior that violates norms and rules of society, and crime is a type of deviant behavior that violates the mores (some of which are violations of formal criminal law).

### How do sociologists conceptualize and explain deviance and crime?

Deviance is behavior that is recognized as violating expected rules and norms and that should be understood in the social context in which it occurs. Psychological explanations of deviance place the cause of deviance primarily within the individual. Sociologists emphasize the total social context in which deviance occurs. Sociologists see deviance more as the result of group and institutional, not individual, behavior.

### What does sociological theory contribute to the study of deviance and crime?

Structural functionalist theory sees both deviance and crime as functional for the society because it affirms what is acceptable by defining what is not.

- Merton's structural strain theory, a type of functionalist theory, predicts that societal inequalities actually force and compel the individual into deviant and criminal behavior.
- Conflict theory explains deviance and crime as a consequence of unequal power relationships and inequality in society.
- Symbolic interaction theory explains deviance and crime as the result of meanings people give to various behaviors.
- Differential association theory, a type of symbolic interaction theory, interprets deviance as behavior learned through social interaction with other deviants.
- Labeling theory, also a type of symbolic interaction theory, argues that societal reactions to behavior produce deviance, with some groups having more power than others to assign deviant labels to people.

### What are the major forms of deviance?

Mental illness, stigma, and substance abuse are major forms of deviance studied by sociologists, although deviance comprises many different forms of behavior. Sociological explanations of mental illness focus on the social context in which mental illness develops and is treated. Social stigmas are attributes that are socially devalued. Substance abuse includes alcohol and drug abuse but is not limited to these two forms.

## What are the connections between inequality, deviance, and crime?

Sociological studies of crime analyze the various types of crimes, such as elite crime, organized crime, corporate crime, and personal and property crimes. Many types of crimes are underreported, such as rape and certain elite and corporate crimes. Sociologists study the conditions, including race, class, and gender inequality, that produce crime and shape how different groups are treated by the criminal justice system, such as showing group differences in sentencing.

## How is crime related to race, class, and gender?

In general, crime rates for a variety of crimes are higher among minorities than among Whites, among poorer persons than among middle or upper-class persons, and among men than among women. Women, especially minority women, are more likely to be victimized by serious crimes such as rape or violence from a spouse or boyfriend.

## How is globalization affecting the development of deviance and crime?

International terrorism is both global and a crime. Today, major terrorist groups like al Qaeda and ISIS not only pose a threat to global security, but through the use of social media, are able to recruit adherents from around the world. Thus, crimes are clearly not just the acts of a crazed individual or small group of individuals, but the result of structural and cultural conditions.

## Section 10: Questions on Religion

### What is religion?

We define religion as a system of symbols, beliefs and practices focused on questions of ultimate meaning.

### According to Durkheim, what are the elements of religion?

Durkheim observed that all religions divide the world into sacred and special realm and a profane or ordinary realm. He suggested that society itself is the true object of worship and that various cultures develop symbolic representations of society.

### What are the functions of religion?

Religion functions to promote social solidarity, strengthen the normative structure of the community, mark life events, and explain life's uncertainties.

### How is religion related to social conflict?

Religion also contributes to bitter and often bloody conflict and a tool of exploitation. Elites use religion to justify their exploitation of the masses and to distract the masses from awareness of this exploitation. As Marx and Engel have shown, religion often helps sustain social class inequality which eventually leads to revolution. Religious groups often fight and divide. Religious figures are frequently found at the front of social movements such as those for civil rights, peace, nuclear disarmament and liberation from the tyranny of dictators.

### What are the types of religion?

The various types of religions hold various objects to be sacred and or supernatural. In simple supernaturalism an impersonal force of nature is regarded as sacred whereas in animism the sacred resides in spirits of the animals and natural phenomena. Totemism is a form of animism in which an animal or plant is worshipped as a god and ancestor. Theistic religions focus attention on a sacred god or gods. Ethical religions focus on principles held to be sacred.

### What are the types of religious organizations?

Religious organizations tend to fall into four types. Ecclesias are state supported whereas denominations are not and must compete with other religious organizations emphasizing lay leadership and a return to the true beliefs of the dominant religion. Cults are often small but they are distinguished primarily with a claim to new revelation often made by a charismatic leader.

**What have sociologists learned about cults?**

Cults typically have not become large denominations. The public is extremely wary about the acts carried out by some cults.

**How has religion become politicized?**

Religious leaders increasingly take political positions.

**What is animism?**

It is a belief that the sacred lives and resides in spirits found in people and other natural phenomena, such as wind and the rain.

**What is a cult?**

Cult is a religious organization that claims a unique new revelation.

**What are ethical religions?**

Religions that do not worship a god as such but rather promote a moral code or belief.

**What are religious symbols?**

Objects, images and words that take meaning from sacred things that they represent and that may become sacred themselves after repeated association.

# Section 11: Questions on Social Stratification

### What is social stratification?

Stratification is a hierarchy of positions with regard to economic production which influences the social rewards to those in the positions.

### What is class?

Class is large set of people regarded by themselves or others as sharing similar status with regard to wealth, power and prestige.

### What are the major forms of stratification?

- Primitive communalism characterized by a high degree of sharing and minimal social inequality.
- Slavery involving great social inequality and the ownership of some persons by others.
- Caste in which an individual is permanently assigned to a status based on his or her parents' status.
- Estate in which peasants are required by law to work land owned by the noble class in exchange for food and protection from outside attacks.

### How do stratification systems differ?

Openness is the opportunity for individuals to change their status. Caste stratification systems are closed whereas class stratification systems are more open. The degree of equality is the degree to which the social structure approaches an equal distribution of resources. Hunting and gathering societies are typically very equal with inequality developing in later stages of agriculture and industrialization.

### What are Weber's three dimensions of stratification?

1. Class or a set of people with similar amounts of income and wealth.
2. Party or a set of people with similar amounts of power.
3. Status group or a set of people with similar social prestige or positive regard from members of a society.

### What are the five basic viewpoints on why stratification exists?

1. Natural inevitability which suggests that inequality exists because of

       natural differences in people's abilities and is a just system.
    2. Structural-functionalist which states that stratification is useful to society because it enhances stability and induces members of the society to work hard.
    3. Conflict which suggests that stratification occurs through conflict between different classes, with the upper classes using superior power to take a larger share of the social resources.
    4. Evolutionary which states that people will share enough resources to ensure the survival of the group until a surplus exists at which time power determines how the surplus is distributed.
    5. Symbolic interactionism, which calls attention to the importance of symbolic displays of wealth and power that influence one's definition of self and the importance of ideas in defining social situations.

**In what regard is some stratification inevitable?**

Inequality may emanate from natural differences in people's abilities.

**What are the functionalist and conflict theories as to the reasons for stratification?**

Structural-functionalists believe that societies tend to be stable and are held together through consensus. Stratification provides an important function to society by aiding this process because it lessens conflict and provides structure. Conflict theorists believe that society tends toward conflict and change and that stratification system coerce the lower classes in order to benefit the upper classes.

**What are the basic premises of the evolutionary perspective?**

In primitive societies, the survival of the group is paramount and people will share their resources to ensure that the group survives. As society develops increasingly sophisticated technology, surplus exists and power will determine the distribution of the surplus.

**How are the supporting beliefs symbolically important to a stratification system?**

Symbolic interactionists point out that symbols help to define the meaning of all social actions, and a person's self is developed socially through social interaction. Legitimating ideas, expressed symbolically in the form of language provide reasons for inequality for strata for the ways people are placed in the strata and for changes in the stratification system. These supporting ideas also strongly affect how people evaluate themselves within the system, influencing

them to accept their position in the structure as good and right.
**What is social mobility?**

Social mobility is the movement of a person from one status to another, either between generations or within a person's adult career.

**What is structural mobility?**

Structural mobility is mobility brought about by changes in the stratification hierarchy for instance as society becomes more technologically advanced.

# Section 12: Questions on Gender Inequality

**What is the difference between sex and gender?**

The term gender refers to culturally transmitted differences between men and women, whereas the sex refers to the biological differences between males and females.

**What do cross-cultural comparisons of gender roles show us?**

Culture largely determines what is considered masculine or feminine. These definitions can change with social change in the culture.

**What are the functionalist and conflict theories of the origin of gender roles?**

Functionalist suggests that men perform instrumental roles and women perform expressive roles because that division is functional to the society. Conflict theory sees the almost universal inequality between the sexes in societies as an outgrowth of patriarchy the form of social organization in which men dominate or rule over women. Patriarchy assumes that men are superior to women based on sexism or the belief that one sex is inferior and thus deserves inferior treatment.

**What are the major socialization agents that teach us our gender roles?**

The major gender role socialization agents are the family, schools, the media and the language, and the observed interactions in the institutions of the culture.

**What are the basic modes in which the family socializes gender behavior?**

The family socializes gender roles through reinforcement of appropriate behaviors, differential opportunities for boys and girls, role modeling of adult gender behavior and explicit verbal instruction.

**What is the relationship between women's work and power in society?**

One reason men hesitate to perform traditional female tasks is that the tasks are often seen as less valuable to society than are traditional male tasks. As a society, we are only beginning to appreciate the economic and social value of homemakers, women or men.

**What political gains have women made?**

More women are entering government from the local to the national level.

**What changes might occur in the second stage of gender relations?**

In the second stage of gender relations, women and men must join together, contributing their own special qualities to building a better society both in the family and in the business world. Women must seek out friendships with other women and learn to value their own contributions to the world.

**What is Jessie Bernard's basic concept concerning the female world?**

Bernard believes that the female world is based on love, cooperation and duty whereas the male world is based on competition and striving. She seeks to sensitize women to the unique contributions the female world view might make to society in order to help it to grow more cooperative and peaceful.

**What is patriarchy?**

It is a form of social organization in which men dominate or rule over women.

**What is sexism?**

It is a belief that one sex is inferior and thus deserves inferior treatment.

# Section 13: Questions on Race and Ethnicity

### What is ethnicity and how is it transmitted?

Ethnicity is a sense of peoplehood or nationhood that is culturally transmitted.

### What is race and how has it been used by societies?

A race is a population that shares visible physical characteristics from inbreeding and that thinks of itself or is thought of by outsiders as distinct. It has been used by societies to justify poor treatment of minority groups.

### What is a minority group?

A minority group is one that has less power and influence than the dominant group.

### What is prejudice?

Prejudice is a judgement based on group membership or social status.

### What is discrimination?

Discrimination involves treating someone differently because of his or her group membership or social status.

### What is the relationship between prejudice and discrimination?

Prejudice and discrimination can exist separately but are most often mutually reinforcing.

### What are the basic patterns of race and ethnic group relations?

The basic patterns of race and ethnic relations are amalgamation (blending two or more groups into a society that reflects the cultural and biological traits of the group), assimilation, pluralism, structured inequality, population relocation and extermination.

### How do conflict theorists define inter group conflict and what are the five major factors that might contribute to it?

When conflict exists between two groups the group that gains the most power, wealth and prestige becomes the majority regardless of its size. The five major factors that contribute to such conflict are visible differences between groups, competition for resources, racist ideology, potential for exploitation and the minority group response to the majority definition of the situation.

**What are some of the possible sources of prejudice and discrimination?**

Prejudice may be formed through both individual and group influences including socialization, rationalizing through stereotypes, the scapegoating process, reinforcement of a self-fulfilling prophecy ramification of an authoritarian personality and degree of contact with minority groups.

Prejudice may be formed through both individual and group influences including socialization, rationalizing through stereotypes, the scapegoating process, reinforcement of a self-fulfilling prophecy ramification of an authoritarian personality and degree of contact with minority groups.

# Section 14: Questions on Collective Behavior and Social Movements

**What are the differences between collective behavior and social movements?**

Collective behavior describes the actions, thoughts and feelings of a relatively temporary and unstructured group of people. In contrast, a social movement is a large ongoing group of people engaged in organized behavior designed to bring about or resist change in society.

**What are the four types of crowd behavior?**
1. The casual crowd gathers around a specific event and its members have little interaction with one another.
2. A conventional crowd gathers for a socially sanctioned purpose.
3. An expressive crowd gathers specifically for the purpose of letting out emotions.
4. An acting crowd focuses on a specific action or goal.

**What do contagion and convergence theories say about crowd behavior?**

LeBon's contagion theory suggests that a collective mind forms in a crowd, which takes over the individual minds of crowd members and causes them to act alike. Convergence theory builds on this by suggesting that crowd members do not really lose their individuality in a group but act from their unconscious selves.

**How do norms emerge in crowd interaction?**

Turner and Killian say that as people interact in a crowd they form new norms for that specific crowd and as the norms emerge; the crowd pressures its members to conform to them.

**When are crowds likely to use violence?**

Crowds are more likely to use violence - rioting when they feel they are being oppressed and wish to overthrow their oppressors.

**How does Neil Smelser explain collective behavior?**

Smelser says six determinants are necessary and sufficient for a collective episode to occur. They are:
1. structural conduciveness
2. structural strain

3. growth and spread of a generalized belief
4. precipitating factors
5. mobilization of participants for action and
6. the operation of social control.

**Under what circumstances does a diffuse crowd form?**

Diffuse crowd or mass behavior involves action by people with common concerns who may or may not have met each other.

**Why do we believe in rumors and how do they affect our actions?**

Rumors are information that travels from person to person usually by word of mouth. As they spread rumors become leveled or simplified and sharpened or focused on certain details. Rumors may be a causal factor in riots. It has been suggested that they are often a substitute for news.

**How do hysteria and panic affect us?**

Hysteria is generalized anxiety about some unknown situation and panic is an attempt to flee from an imagined or real threat. Often this can create behavior changes in individuals. From illness caused by an imagined bug to flight out of town in response to an imagined invasion from Mars.

**What is the difference between fashions and fads?**

Fashions and fads are changing styles currently accepted by a part of the population but which are not considered a permanent part of the culture. Fashions change more gradually than fads.

**What are the major influences on public opinion?**

A public is an unorganized diffuse crowd with opinions on an issue of current interest. Public opinion is influenced in two major ways: by friends or reference groups and by members of that group whose judgement is considered important opinion leaders.

**How does the mass media influence other social phenomena?**

The national media strongly influence the formation of public opinion. They may also be a catalyst in social explosions such as riots. The fact that programming is now immediate leads to less sorting of what is important and what is not and may actually distort reality for the viewer.

**What is the relationship between television and suicide?**

David Philips and Lundie Carstensen determined that in the specific case of teenage suicide, media violence causes audience violence. They found that television news or feature stories about suicides triggered additional teenage suicides because of imitation.

**What are four types of social movements?**
1. Resistance movements are formed to resist a change that is already occurring in society.
2. Reform movements endeavor to change elements of the system as it currently stands.
3. Revolutionary movements deny that the system will ever work and seek to replace it.
4. Expressive movements concentrate on change among their members and their immediate social contacts.

**How do social movements become professionalized?**

It has been suggested that many social movements today have leaders whose primary function is to organize and obtain funds and support for a movement thus making it a highly centralized organization run by professionals.

**What are the stages in the life of a social movement?**

In the preliminary stage, society shows a restless concern over an issue on which people are divided. In the popular stage the movements begins to rally around a charismatic leader who speaks for reform, revolution, resistance or expression of self in such a way that people relate to the leader and begin to feel hopeful that their questions have answers. In the third stage, it destroys itself as a movement and becomes an institution with all the organized and accepted norms of society.

# Section 15: Questions on the Family

### What are the sociological definitions of marriage and the family?

Marriage is a long term socially approved sexual union between two people. Marriage usually forms the basis of a family; two or more generations of people related by marriage, birth or adoption, who live together and share economic resources.

### How do societies control love and marriage?

Societies control love and marriage through rules about marriage partners including kinship ties, locality and isolation of pubescent.

### What are the functions of the family as a social institution?

The family controls human reproduction, caring for dependents, socialization of children and intimate relationships.

### What are the conflict and functionalist views of families and social stratification?

Functionalists see the family's role in transmitting social status as natural and valuable. Conflict theorists see it as an agent of inequality and an impediment to reform.

### What are some of the major disadvantages of the nuclear family?

The nuclear family has an inherent lack of extended support system, instability and a vulnerability to economic stress.

### How is violence seen in the family context?

Although families are usually considered positive social groups, recent research has uncovered rampant violence in the family from the spouse abuse to sexual and physical and mental/emotional abuse of children. This violence crosses class boundaries and is found in virtually all types of families.

### How does divorce affect the family members?

Divorced men and women show great signs of emotional stress: high suicide rates, loss of jobs and seeking psychiatric treatment. Divorced mothers will likely struggle against poverty whereas divorced fathers struggle against loneliness. Children show symptoms from anxiety to drug abuse and poor school performance.

**What is exogamy?**

It is a marriage form in which spouses must come from outside the social group.

**What is the difference between family of orientation and family of procreation?**

Family of orientation is the nuclear family we are born into, our parents and siblings. Family of procreation is the family we create by marrying and becoming partners.

Made in the USA
Coppell, TX
13 December 2019